The
CLEVELAND
GRAND PRIX
An American Show Jumping First

Betty
WEIBEL

*To Lukeisha,
Enjoy the book!
Betty Weibel*

Charleston London

THE
History
PRESS

Published by The History Press
Charleston, SC 29403
www.historypress.net

First published 2014

Manufactured in the United States

ISBN 978.1.62619.525.7

Library of Congress CIP data applied for.

This book is dedicated to all of the volunteers and horsemen who worked over the past fifty years to make the Cleveland Grand Prix a success. Their hard work and passionate dedication created generations of fans and added to the rich culture of the Chagrin Valley. And it is written for one special fan in particular: Nancy.

CONTENTS

Contents

Acknowledgements

There is no greater agony than bearing an untold story inside you.
—Maya Angelou

Many people contributed to making this book possible, and Karen Schneider leads the list for helping in so many ways, including climbing storage locker ladders, digging through musty archive boxes and endless fact-checking. Other major sources of information and assistance were Charles Kinney, Mary Silcox of Stadium Jumping Inc., Marty Bauman and Meg Schermerhorn of Classic Communications and Ken Kraus.

The author thanks the following for taking time to share their stories and details: Laddie Andahazy, Mary Chapot, Dan Collister, Peter Doubleday, Leonard King, Howard Lewis, Gene Mische, Michael Morrissey, Betty Oare, Tom Visconsi, William Steinkraus and, from the United States Cavalry Association, Frederick Klink, Walter J. Schweitzer and his daughter Karen McMannon. Books, newspapers, horse show programs and interviews with directly involved sources helped confirm the countless facts and abundant information collected for this book.

Thanks to the photographers who captured the Cleveland Grand Prix over the years on behalf of the Chagrin Valley PHA Horse Show Inc. Some of their work is displayed in this book: Bruce Wilkinson, George Axt, Marshall Hawkins, Leslie Howard, Judy Buck, Paul Tepley, O'Neils, Laura Simon, Vesty Photography, Sandy Lee, Father James F. Flood, Flying Horse Photography, Tish Quirk, Anne Gittins and Ohio Photographers. Thanks also to the public relations professionals and media who supported the show and grand prix and chronicled events over the years, particularly Roland Kraus, who was involved in both promoting the Cleveland Grand Prix and reporting on horse sports in Northeast Ohio for the *Plain Dealer*, and reporter Marge Fernbacher.

The author also thanks Pat Zalba and Zo Sykora of Chagrin Falls Historical Society, Sally Burke and Gates Mills Historical Society and Museum, Annmarie Kasper of the Chagrin Valley Hunt Club, Ann Sindelar from Western Reserve Historical Society, Kathleen Landwehr of the United States Equestrian Federation, Mollie Bailey and the staff at *The Chronicle of the Horse* and Cami Blanchard and her team at Lake Erie College.

Special thanks to my behind-the-scenes team: Heather Lampman, Esther Morgan, Linda Henry, Stephanie Groff, Michelle Wood and Claire Weibel.

When local and equine publishers initially failed to show interest, Christine Brune, executive director of American Horse Publications, came to the rescue and introduced me to the wonderful team at The History Press and my commissioning editor, Greg Dumais.

Special thanks to my family for their support and encouragement—my husband David, my parents and brothers, Myrna Weibel and especially my daughter Claire, who edited countless drafts, outlines and proposals and inspired and encouraged me.

INTRODUCTION

If you want to understand today, you have to search yesterday.
—Pearl Buck

Northeast Ohio earned a reputation as a hub in the horse world and was an incubator for the fledgling sport of American grand prix horse show jumping. Cleveland was home to successful inventors, business leaders and titans of industry, and for many of them, leisure time revolved around their passion for horse sports. This passion created an ideal environment that encouraged competition and innovation, which ultimately boosted show jumping to new heights.

In order to appreciate the significance of the sport of grand prix show jumping and its birth in Ohio's Chagrin Valley, it is important to understand the environment that laid the groundwork for development and expansion of horse sports. Local history became intertwined with the evolution of American show jumping when Clevelanders' idea for a grand prix–style competition grew from the need to be competitive with European equestrians, who outnumbered and out-jumped their North American counterparts.

The first North American show jumping grand prix for civilian amateur and professional riders was held in 1965. The Cleveland Grand Prix introduced European-style show jumping in the United States at a time when the new United States Equestrian Team, formed post-cavalry, was focusing its attention on fielding strong teams for Nation's Cups, Olympic games and other international competition. The domestic training ground for these athletes was limited, as was the depth of experienced horses and riders capable of challenging foreign show jumpers.

When North American competitors were introduced to the grand prix concept of show jumping at the Cleveland Grand Prix, the enormous size of the obstacles, the length of the course and the wide water jump were all new to American horsemen. Some reacted by protesting the course and threatened to withdraw because they felt it was too difficult and dangerous. The $3,000 prize money purse, the largest ever offered up to that time, provided encouragement to take the risk and compete.

On competition day, the riders negotiated the course safely and discovered that although it was difficult, it wasn't impossible. The Cleveland Grand Prix gave horsemen a new level to aspire to, and it gave the North American spectators a thrilling new sport to watch.

The Cleveland Grand Prix was one of more than fifty different classes held during the July Chagrin Valley PHA Horse Show, but it outshined them all and attracted more than fifty thousand fans. The horse show and its new grand prix finale impacted the local economy and launched a national equestrian industry around show jumping.

For more than fifty years, horses and their teams of riders, owners and support staff from across the country and beyond the U.S. borders have traveled to the Chagrin Valley for the annual horse show. The transformation of the peaceful park polo field into an international competition arena was not unlike watching the circus come to town and set up its show. Ohio was significant in the equestrian world for hosting one of the largest hunter/jumper shows in the country and attracting the best of the best as they traveled the show circuit competing for year-end honors.

For the professional seasoned rider, success at the Chagrin Valley PHA Horse Show was a major career boost. For aspiring young amateur riders, it was a way to get noticed, especially if they were interested in being considered for a spot on the United States Equestrian Team. For the horse owner, a blue ribbon at the Chagrin Valley PHA Horse Show could translate into financial gain in the future sale of a horse. Even after the sport grew and the number of grand prix multiplied, the prestigious Cleveland Grand Prix remained the original—the one to win.[1]

When the first grand prix was conceived in 1965, it launched new traditions and careers in the show jumping world. The involvement of hundreds of horsemen, financial supporters and hardworking board members and volunteers brought the dream to reality. The results impacted equestrian sport worldwide, as well as the local economy, Cleveland's history and the lives of those involved in the event. As the Cleveland Grand Prix matured, it elevated the caliber of U.S. riders and added to the rich fabric of the Chagrin Valley.

The lure of the Cleveland Grand Prix united Ohioans from all walks of life, from the wealthiest business leaders to humble horsemen without a dollar in the bank. As a young spectator, the exciting jumping attracted me year after year. Watching the Cleveland Grand Prix was magical—like seeing celebrities on horseback with the nation's best horses and riders in our own backyard. My friends Linda and Lorrie Huefner and I waited all year for that day to come. Afterward, I went home to imagine jumping big fences as I rode school horses in weekly riding lessons.

I never thought I would one day work on publicity for the Chagrin Valley PHA Horse Show or co-chair the event. That is when I really learned that the horse show was more than a collection of competitive classes and divisions that group horses and riders by common characteristics. Behind the scenes, it is a patchwork quilt of stories and experiences of passionate people who worked hard to bring new ideas to the sport while preserving important traditions. They continue to work hard on the horse show today to keep it alive and preserve its grand finale, the legendary Cleveland Grand Prix, a tradition that defines the culture of the Chagrin Valley.

This horse show isn't about the quest for a piece of satin ribbon. It is a life event that brings people together for a common passion of horses, whether they are riders, trainers, grooms, volunteers, sponsors, spectators or conducting other business. For those involved, it is a defining factor in their lifestyle that is dictated by commitment and dedication in preparing year-round for the big event—not unlike Santa and his elves preparing for Christmas Day!

Today, the horse world is changing, and show jumping continues to evolve. Horse shows are consolidating and dwindling based on the economy and expenses involved with the sport and running an event. The number of grand prix has grown to about 350 as of this writing, and competition for the shrinking pool of sponsor dollars is fierce. Will the Chagrin Valley PHA Horse Show and its Cleveland Grand Prix continue on?

Part I

WHY CLEVELAND?

Chapter 1

THE EARLY YEARS:
HORSES IN CLEVELAND SPORTS

That a city like Cleveland, possessing so many advantages, and representing so much wealth, should allow herself to fall behind her sister cities in any progressive or wide-awake movement, is of course out of the question—therefore, Cleveland is to have a Horse Show; not simply because it is the fashion, but because such amusements create genuine enthusiasm, give those possessing riches an idea as to how they may spend their money to good advantage, and excite a (harmless) rivalry in the matter of saddle horses, and turnouts generally. Everyone wants the best—therefore, the standard is put high.

Where one sees (as is too often the case) a fine pair of Cobs, endowed with style and action, driven as though they were in reality but one removed from their overworked brother of the vendor wagon. To bring out the fine points of any horse, he must be driven and ridden intelligently. In too many cases the horse has the advantage of his driver in intelligence and common-sense. Therefore, it is not enough to own fine horses; one must know how to drive them, or know how they should be driven. There has also been a marked change and improvement in the line of equestrianism. Slow too, but sure. Young and old are beginning to realize not only the delightful exhilaration which is inseparable from horseback riding, but also its marvelously healthful effects, and it needs only a short trial to prove those laboring under almost any bodily infirmity, that they can safely "throw physic to the dogs."
—Preface, 1893 Cleveland Riding Academy souvenir program

Northeast Ohio, from Cleveland to the eastern countryside known as the Chagrin Valley, earned its reputation as an important nucleus of the horse world. Situated on the shores of Lake Erie, Cleveland is the largest city in Northeast Ohio, and its history is linked to the development of horses in sport. Although the equine partner was originally a true workhorse used for utilitarian and transportation purposes, that role transitioned with the city.

Horses were laborers, but they doubled in frontier sports such as plowing matches that tested the best. The first county fair in the area was held in 1829 on Public Square in Cleveland and featured livestock exhibitions, as well as match races. Residents from all walks of life enjoyed the friendly community competitions with their neighbors.

Racing didn't stop in the winter. It continued in the form of popular community sleigh meets, where towns competed to see who could have the best turnout. In 1856, Medina County won the contest with 185 sleighs.[2] Cleveland—a town of invention and innovation—was at the heart of the Industrial Revolution. With success and wealth, Clevelanders invested in their leisure passions, and during that time, those passions included horses. Horse sports flourished in the form of fine carriages, harness and flat racing and the nation's best show horses.

Horses and horse sports were a passion of the day, as well as a way for wealthy Clevelanders to compete against their peers. A number of great

Four-in-Hand coach traffic in Cleveland, 1907. *Western Reserve Historical Society.*

sportsmen shaped American horse sports. In doing so, they left their mark on the culture of Cleveland.

In 1887, Clevelander J.B. Perkins was importing Hackney horses from England, as they were America's most popular carriage horse in pre-automotive times. He hired an Irishman, Hugh O'Neill, as his coachman and to benefit from his talent in understanding horses to purchase. Perkins, a leader in the equestrian community, organized the Bit and Bridle Club in 1888 for exercise and camaraderie. Among the wealthy Clevelanders who enjoyed equestrian pursuits such as sleigh racing were John D. Rockefeller, John Hay, Myron Herrick, Harry Devereaux and Charles Otis, and many of them turned to O'Neill for equine advice.[3]

Within the city of Cleveland, winter races ran down the main streets. Sometimes thirty to forty sleighs raced along Euclid Avenue's Millionaire's Row, and thousands lined the streets to watch drivers representing the city's first families: Rockefeller, Hanna, Perkins and Corning.[4] If you weren't a participant in horse sport, you were likely a spectator.

O'Neill went on to start his own livery business in the early 1900s and later operated Cleveland's horse-drawn garbage collection service and newspaper delivery service. At a time when businesses were converting to the automotive industry, O'Neill was one of the last Cleveland

Sleigh racing down Cleveland's Euclid Avenue. *Western Reserve Historical Society.*

businessmen to use horses for commercial purposes. Horses became too slow for making newspaper deliveries, and Northeast Ohio's severe winters caused major delays. O'Neill converted the horse-drawn fleet to motorized trucking by the 1920s.[5] That humble beginning and inspirational success story resulted in one of the nation's largest trucking companies, Leaseway Transportation Corporation.

Horse Racing Booms

The summer season focused on a different kind of racing—harness racing with trotters. And it became harder for average citizens to win because better horses cost more money. On the east side of the city, the Glenville Race Track was built in 1870 by the Cleveland Driving Park Company as part of the Northern Ohio Fair. The regional meets featured locally bred horses and nationally ranked trotters such as William H. Vanderbilt's Maud S. Some of the top harness racing horses in the country were bred or trained in Cleveland.[6]

The track scene was also a social setting with elegantly attired women and men watching from carriages, some of whom were members of the Four-in-

The Cuyahoga County Fairgrounds, Chagrin Falls. *Chagrin Falls Historical Society.*

Horse racing in Chagrin Falls in the 1920s. *Chagrin Falls Historical Society.*

Hand Tandem Club, a local club for driving enthusiasts. Entourages of fine carriages pulled by matching teams were announced by coach horns when they visited the racetrack to spectate. Eventually, the one-mile oval horse track became the site of major automotive races.

In 1873, the Union Fair Association was organized for the purpose of improving the quality of horseflesh raised for racing trotters, pacers and runners.[7] The organization leased Chagrin Falls land for the Cuyahoga County Fair, which was in need of a new home, and the fair remained there until it moved to Berea in 1925. The grounds included a half-mile track, a wooden grandstand, stabling, fencing and an exhibit hall on what is today the grounds of the Chagrin Falls High School.

In 1920, the Chagrin Falls Jockey Club was organized, and it hosted Thoroughbred racing at the rented fairgrounds site. Additional improvements to the track and grounds attracted top horses from Cuba, Mexico and the United States. However, racing in Chagrin Falls made headlines for the wrong reason, as gambling and track betting were illegal in Ohio. Racing was eventually halted when a "no betting" judicial order dispatched sheriff's deputies to close the track.[8]

Horse racing eventually moved to the track in North Randall and its sister track, Thistledown, which opened in 1925.

The Cleveland Cavalry

Horses played important roles as equine partners in Cleveland's cavalry. The lawlessness that attended the great railroad strike was the direct cause of a meeting in 1877 to discuss the advisability of forming a troop of cavalry. In October 1877, the First City Troop of Cleveland, forerunner of Troop A, was formed with Colonel William H. Harris as captain, Brevet Brigadier General E.S. Meyer as first lieutenant and Colonel George A. Garretson as second lieutenant. Two years later, the troop's first armory was built on Euclid Avenue.[9]

The troop operated under several banners over the years: Troop A of the First Cleveland Cavalry/107th Cavalry, the First City Troop and Ohio National Guard. The independent military company was formed with the purpose of preserving law and order. One of the early objectives of members was to perfect their horsemanship knowledge and use of arms through weekly drills and military exercises. Standard military training incorporated exercises from horse sports—jumping hurdles, playing polo, steeplechase racing and the precision riding of dressage. There were a number of troops making up the Ohio regiment of cavalry, and a healthy rivalry existed between them. Beginning in 1912, a pennant was awarded during the annual encampments to the most efficient troop. On nearly every occasion, the pennant was won by Troop A of Cleveland.

Troop A cavalry camp in Novelty, Ohio. *Western Reserve Historical Society.*

The troop served in a number of ceremonial functions, including escorting governors and presidents and marching in inaugurations and funerals. Troop A was also placed on alert several times and called into action in 1899 in Cleveland during the Streetcar Strike; troop members escorted cars down the streets and stood guard around the city. They were also called into service during the tobacco wars in southern Ohio in 1908, a Columbus streetcar strike in 1910, after the Fremont floods in 1913 and following a tornado in Lorain in 1924.

During World War I, Troop A and the Ohio Regiment of Cavalry became a field artillery unit and saw action in France, losing five members in combat. The troop left federal service in 1919 and rejoined the Ohio National Guard as Troop A, 107th Cavalry. Eventually, cutbacks in the U.S. Department of Defense resulted in the unit being officially deactivated in 1993.[10]

The first armory that housed the troop in Cleveland lacked enough space for the horses, so the trustees of the Troop A Veterans Association developed a plan to build a new armory with space for a large riding school that would provide training for the public and generate income for the troop. The new

Riding instructor Laddie Andahazy. *Lake Erie College.*

First Cleveland Cavalry Troop A emblem, 1877. *Author's collection.*

Troop A Riding Academy and Armory was built in Shaker Heights in 1923. The property was planned with room for exhibitions, horse shows and polo matches. Troop A was an important inspiration to many local equestrians, including some of the country's top horsemen. Among the riding instructors were Dick Lavery and Laddie Andahazy, who conducted large group lessons for the public. Riding was a growing sport, and many people wanted to develop the skill, even if they didn't own a horse. Andahazy was also pivotal in developing the Lake Erie College equestrian program and, later, the first Cleveland Grand Prix. Clevelander Eugene Mische lived near the armory and confessed to sneaking in the back door as a youth to watch the riding lessons. Later, he rode at the armory and gained the experience needed to embark on a successful career as a trainer and horse show pioneer.

The locations changed, and the final two-story brick-and-steel armory facility at Kemper and Fairhill Roads remained in use until the 1960s, when the Veterans Association sold it. Later, the Cleveland Skating Club took over the building, and today a Cavalry Room at the private club pays tribute to the early cavalrymen with a collection of mementos and photos. Among the displays are early jumping trophies and a Cleveland Horse Show program from the Central Armory dated November 8–12, 1898. Hanging on the wall is a 1922 sponsorship solicitation letter penned by Captain J.B. Perkins and requesting financial support from local retailer the Higbee Company to help fund the new riding academy.

Not only did the Cleveland cavalry serve the community, but it also served an important role in developing local horsemen and stimulating the local equestrian industry. Across America, the U.S. Cavalry influenced modern American show jumping by providing a training ground for future horsemen and Olympians.

Chapter 2

THE CHAGRIN VALLEY:
LAND FOR HORSE SPORTS

A s Cleveland prospered, the population swelled, and the city became the fifth largest in the country. Development of the outlying suburbs was slow initially due to limited transportation that depended on horse-drawn wagons, carts and coaches over rutted dirt roads, which made travel uncomfortable. The Chagrin Falls and Cleveland Stage & Express was the regularly scheduled mode of transportation, leaving Chagrin Falls in the early morning and returning from Cleveland in the evening.

In 1897, the Cleveland and Eastern Railroad built an interurban railroad, making transport to the east a mere hour's ride. The Chagrin Valley suburbs of Chagrin Falls, Gates Mills and Hunting Valley became excursion destinations for city dwellers. Property including small farms in eastern Cuyahoga County were sold or rented as wealthy Clevelanders purchased second homes with acreage that afforded them access to a broader sporting life. With little or no income tax and a booming economy, the captains of industry amassed fortunes in oil, lake shipping, coal, steelmaking and other manufacturing. Many turned their leisure interests to horses, having cultivated a passion from European traditions and visits to Maryland and Virginia, where they enjoyed the sport of fox hunting.

In the early 1900s, the Interurban Railroad provided transportation between Cleveland and Chagrin Falls. *Chagrin Falls Historical Society.*

Fox Hunting in the Valley

The beautiful Chagrin Valley was popular with horsemen seeking open fields suitable for hacking and hunting, as well as open roads for coach rides. One horseman, Edward Merritt, drove his horse-drawn rigs along the rutted dirt roads, and his positive relationship with local farmers helped pave the way for riding across lands. He was active in the Cleveland Four-in-Hand and Tandem Club that was formed in the early 1900s.[11]

In the late 1890s, a group of riders hunted over farmland as part of the Cleveland Hunt and the Cuyahoga Cross Country Riding Association. Led by industrialist Charles Otis, they made their home base at the Maple Leaf Inn in Gates Mills. In 1909, they moved forward with the purchase of the inn, stables and property that became known as the Chagrin Valley Hunt Club. Their first meet was held that year when Windsor T. White led a ride across the Chagrin Valley countryside in and around Gates Mills.[12]

Located eighteen miles east of Cleveland, the club was attended by many of Cleveland's prominent families, including Windsor and Walter White

Thanksgiving Day drag hunt with the Chagrin Valley Hunt, 1908. *Gates Mills Historical Society.*

(pioneer manufacturers of autos and sewing machines), bankers Edmund S. Burke Jr. and Corliss Sullivan, steelmaker Elroy J. Kulas, attorney Frank Ginn, industrialist Amasa Stone Mather, banker-diplomat Myron T. Herrick, accountant A.C. Ernst, aviator and naval undersecretary David S. Ingalls, the Van Sweringen brothers and others.

Polo in the Valley

The Chagrin Valley Hunt Club offered a very sophisticated program of horse activities involving show horses, polo teams and riding to the hounds. At that time, virtually every club member was active in horse activities. Polo teams, often made up of all one family—the Whites, Knutsens, Baldwins, Firestones—competed all over the world and won. We entertained polo teams from Mexico and South America, often army officers still wearing their guns, and, of course, this required lavish entertaining of the distinguished guests.
—Dan Collister, former Gates Mills mayor, during a 2012 speech at a Gates Mills Historical Society gathering

A polo match at the Hunting Valley field. *Chagrin Falls Historical Society.*

Polo was introduced to the area in 1911 at Edmund Burke Jr.'s Wickliffe farm.[13] Sometimes referred to as croquet on horseback, the sport required space, and several regulation two-hundred- by three-hundred-foot fields were developed over time, which allowed rotation of playing fields.

The Chagrin Valley Hunt Club sponsored matches at its field around 1912, while other players began acquiring land to build their own fields. Windsor White's Halfred Farms and his brother Walter White's Circle W. Farm both hosted prominent competitions, including U.S. Polo League matches and national polo championships. Crowds turned out to see the sport, and attendance was recorded at eight thousand spectators.

To accommodate crowds and traffic, in 1931, the village of Hunting Valley, with funding by the Van Sweringen brothers, built its own polo field with space for spectators and cars to line the field at the corner of newly relocated Kinsman (Route 87) and Chagrin River Roads. Official U.S. Polo Association weekend matches were held at the field and started with a parade of polo ponies led by grooms down River Road, followed by limousines carrying the players. The matches began at 3:30 p.m. at the Hunting Valley Field. The public location made the sport of polo more accessible to all classes of people. Members of society sat under canopies of reserved boxes, while other fans with passes sat on the hoods of Packard, Cadillac and LaSalle cars lining the field.[14]

Cleveland Metroparks Polo Field

The Hunting Valley Polo Field became part of the public park system during a period of growth and expansion of Cleveland's open land and green space. The oldest park district in Ohio, the Cleveland Metropolitan Park District, grew out of a plan for an outer chain of parks with connecting boulevards around Cleveland known as the Emerald Necklace.

By the 1940s, one of the last links to be completed was a parkway between the North Chagrin Reservation in Gates Mills and the South Chagrin Reservation near Chagrin Falls. Hunting Valley Council members eventually agreed to make provisions for a public park. According to the Cleveland Metroparks, they purchased 60.87 acres, including the polo field, for just over $28,000.[15]

The renamed Cleveland Metroparks Polo Field is located at the southeast corner of Chagrin River Road and South Woodland Road. The Chagrin River flows through the middle of the grounds. Some historians attribute the river's name to the French trader Francois Saguin because by 1760, French travelers were calling the Chagrin River "a Seguin," and early maps label the river "Shaguin." Others believed "Shaguin" was an Indian word meaning "clear water." The true origin of the name "Chagrin" remains a mystery.[16]

Today, local polo clubs still play occasional matches at the Cleveland Metroparks Polo Field. Events such as dog shows can be held at the facility after receiving a permit, and it is also home to the Chagrin Valley PHA Horse Show.

Chapter 3

HORSE SHOWS EVOLVE IN NORTHEAST OHIO

Horse shows were the ultimate showcase for equine breeding accomplishments and equestrian talent in riding and driving events. Individuals were judged by a knowledgeable and respected official in their discipline and were measured against their peers. It was fitting that some of Cleveland's earliest horse shows were hosted by the riding academies where people learned their skills, sometimes on borrowed horses. Cleveland horse show programs from the late 1800s (such as the one referenced at the start of Chapter 1) document shows held by the Cleveland Riding Academy and the Troop A Riding Academy.

In 1909, the Chagrin Valley Hunt Club in Gates Mills launched what would become a long-standing tradition with its annual horse show: the Chagrin Valley Hunt Saddle Horse Show. This first show was held on the Case School athletic field, and all subsequent shows were held on club grounds. The two-day show was a success, although newspapers reported that the jumping was chaotic because the horses, accustomed to negotiating obstacles in the hunt field, seemed confused by having to jump in an enclosed riding ring.

Luckily, attendance was low for that first show, so witnesses were few. Hunters competed in various divisions, and the primary course consisted of four hurdles jumped twice around the ring. Riders competed in classes for both individuals and teams, and the second day of the show brought improvement in the performances.[17]

An early Chagrin Valley Hunt Club horse show. *Gates Mills Historical Society*.

A competitor at the Chagrin Valley Hunt Club show lands over the fence before his horse. *Gates Mills Historical Society*.

The final event featured all of the winning hunters and jumpers to determine the champion hunter. First prize and the English silver beaker went to Halfred, ridden and owned by Windsor White. White was also reserve champion aboard Percy Green. Today, his name heads the champion roster posted on the walls of the Chagrin Valley Hunt Club.

In his 2012 speech at the Gates Mills Historical Society, former Gates Mills mayor Dan Collister recalled:

The Hunt Club had the advantage of having areas for both shows and polo. For horse shows, the big field was ideal to form an enclosed ring. This was surrounded by private boxes for viewing, under canvas awnings for shade, with room to park cars right behind the boxes. Horses jumped out of the ring and proceeded around a course similar to open hunting country. Classes for teams of three horses featured identically dressed riders in hunt attire and wearing hats and black jackets with the colors of the hunt club they belonged to across the back of the collar. There was a square leather sandwich case strapped on the side of the saddle—complete with sandwich and flask of sherry, in case the judge checked. They jumped around the course single file. Show horses here competed all over the East—Bryn Mawr, Sewickley, Devon, Piping Rock—and even won Grand Championships at Madison Square Garden in 1938 and 1939. And horses from those areas competed here, all to gain points to go to the year-end championship at Madison Square Garden.

Horse shows were not exclusive to the Chagrin Valley, and competitors traveled to downtown Cleveland for indoor venues such as the Cleveland Public Auditorium. The Cleveland Spring Horse Show was held June 4–7, 1930, and featured events for driving horses such as the Hackney breeding classes, as well as classes ridden under saddle for gaited saddle horses, hunters and jumpers. Mrs. Carl Hanna was among the driving entries, while jumper riders included such names as shipping magnate Crispin Oglebay and Miss Elizabeth Eaton, daughter of industrialist Cyrus Eaton. The Troop A Riding Academy Company also fielded entries in a number of divisions.[18]

Although the downtown horse shows didn't continue, they proved a good training ground for horses, riders and even show officials. One of the officers of the Spring Horse Show was Edward King, who was listed in the program as horse show secretary. He gained valuable experience and went on to become longtime manager of the National Horse Show at Madison Square Garden and a Show Jumping Hall of Fame inductee.[19]

1930 champions Pansy Ireland and Mighty at the Chagrin Valley Hunt Club horse show. *Gates Mills Historical Society.*

Growing interest in horse shows led to a demand for more riding lessons. Lake Erie College in Painesville, Ohio, had been offering riding as a physical education credit since 1928 and figured prominently in the development of show jumping. Paul Weaver became president of Lake Erie College in 1951 and made history as the first college in the United States to require students to spend an academic term abroad. In 1955, Cleveland riding instructor and horseman Laddie Andahazy joined the college. Starting with twelve horses and a small stable on campus, Andahazy made the program a success. By 1967, one hundred of the school's six hundred students were regular participants in equestrian classes. With the support of local donors, the George M. Humphrey Equestrian Center officially opened in 1971.[20]

Other area businesses contributed to the Northeast Ohio equestrian population and benefitted along the way. Red Raider Camp in Russell Township began in 1943 when Shaker Heights physical education teacher Ralston Fox Smith leased land and later purchased it to start a camp for boys and girls. The facility grew to include three barns with one hundred horses. The afternoon riding program averaged more than five hundred students a week during the school year, and the summer camp hosted six hundred campers at a time, including such noted campers as actor Paul Newman. Fox Smith and his wife, Billie, ran the camp until his death in 1975.[21] Roosevelt-Firebird Stables in Perry had a similarly popular riding program with separate boys' and girls' summer camps.

Whether you wanted to compete, ride for pleasure or spectate, the Chagrin Valley had something for everyone.

The Chagrin Valley Trails and Riding Horse Show at the Polo Field

In 1946, Irene Skuse Tripp invited some of her friends to a meeting to form the Chagrin Valley Trails and Riding Club (CVTRC), and the club continues today. The organization of friends and horsemen makes its headquarters at the historic red brick house at the corner of Chagrin River and South Woodland Roads, near the entrance to the Cleveland Metroparks Polo Field. A plaque on the front porch pays tribute to Skuse. The club's mission states: "The Chagrin Valley Trails and Riding Club encourages land conservation, horsemanship, safety and family activities through trail riding in the Chagrin River Valley."

Membership was open to anyone with a horse, and there was a modest initiation fee and equally modest annual dues. The focus was pleasure trail riding rather than competition. As of this writing, the club continues to host events from spring to fall, culminating with a holiday dinner and dance. The house and its spacious deck overlooking the polo field have been the scene of many parties. Maintaining the clubhouse has been an ongoing project, and painting parties and cleanups have been regular activities for the members.

In 1949, an important tradition began at the Cleveland Metroparks Polo Field when the Chagrin Valley Trails and Riding Club launched its annual two-day, all-breed English and Western style horse show as its primary fundraiser. The club was responsible for bringing electricity to the polo field to accommodate the night shows and concessions that supported the show.

The setting for the Chagrin Valley horse show is an important element in the show's success as well as its challenges. The show grounds is part of the Cleveland Metroparks South Chagrin Reservation, and the setting is stunningly beautiful; it is like no other horse show location in the nation.

The grounds sit on a lush green blanket of grass surrounded by trees in a valley that reflects the light and beauty of nature. The Chagrin River flows alongside the polo field, and the land sits in portions of Hunting Valley and Moreland Hills.

The Cleveland Metroparks Polo Field was home to other horse shows over the years, such as the Orange Patronnaires Horse Show, which merged with the FOSP (Friends of St. Paul) spring horse show. However, the show started by the Chagrin Valley Trails and Riding Club was the only one to continue over the years.

Although the horse show offered classes for carriage driving, western riders and gaited horses in the early years, the primary focus was competition for hunters and jumpers. Then as now, hunters compete over jumping obstacles simulating those found in the hunting field like gates, brush, walls and coups. They are judged subjectively on the style, pace and manner of jumping. They are also judged as a group "on the flat" (without jumping), performing the walk, trot and canter. Horses and ponies are grouped by division based on the experience of the horse and/or rider.

Jumpers are judged based on their ability to clear the obstacles and the speed with which they do so. The obstacles tend to be larger and more colorful, and the courses challenge both horses and riders. Fans know exactly who is in the lead, as penalty points are announced when faults occur on course, and the time is posted. Competition is exciting when speed is an added factor, particularly in the case of a tie-breaking jump-off against the clock. Hunter/jumper judging has been compared to ice skating for laymen. The hunters are judged on style, similar to figure skaters, while jumpers are scored on penalties, more like hockey.

The horse show became increasingly popular, and by the 1950s, the members of the club questioned how they would keep up with its need for manpower, time and talent. By the 1960s, the show had evolved to focus its competition as a prestigious hunter/jumper show, attracting exhibitors and spectators to the beautiful polo field setting. It was considered one of the largest outdoor shows in the nation. Among the out-of-town attendees was C.F. Johnson's Fairfield Farms Stable of Lake City, Florida, which was managed by Gene Mische, who brought a number of horses ridden by Rodney Jenkins.

The 1964 horse show program lists the dates July 23–26 for the fifteenth annual Chagrin Valley Trails and Riding Club Show. The chairman of the show was William A. Mattie, and Mr. C.P. Wright was president of the board of directors of the Chagrin Valley Trails and Riding Club. The

1964 Chagrin Valley Trails and Riding Club horse show program cover painted by local artist Paul Meunier. *Chagrin Valley PHA Horse Shows Inc.*

beneficiary of the show was the United States Equestrian Team, which had been founded fifteen years earlier.[22]

The horse show had reached a point that the organizers decided was far beyond their club mission. They did not want to continue in their demanding roles and were looking for new leaders to step up and take over. Fortunately, they didn't have to look too far, as the new leaders were already involved with the show.

In 1964, Charles Mapes was a member of the Prize List Committee, and his wife, Dorothy, was on the Entry Committee; both were members of the club's board of directors. Mrs. Leah Goetz (later Stroud) was listed as secretary of the Chagrin Valley Trails and Riding Club Board of Directors.

The Professional Horsemen's Association of America (PHA) was a self-contained benevolent organization founded in Connecticut in 1936. The PHA was devoted to giving aid to needy horsemen in the form of financial

Professional Horsemen's Association logo. *Author's collection.*

assistance and scholarships, as well as promoting the horse industry and care and protection of horses. Cleveland-area horsemen formed a local chapter of the national organization and included the initials in the name of their horse show, the Chagrin Valley PHA.

Mapes and Goetz, as well as a number of other volunteers, were willing to continue working on the new horse show. The newly formed Chagrin Valley Professional Horsemen's Association (PHA), formerly the Cleveland PHA, was established and took over management and responsibility for the horse show under the new name the Chagrin Valley PHA Horse Show.

The Chagrin Valley PHA Horse Show

Already well known as a top horse show announcer, Charles "Chuck" Mapes became the chairman of the Chagrin Valley PHA Horse Show in 1965, in the midst of a major transition. Mapes had started in the horse world as a groom and operated a small tack shop in Chesterland, Ohio. In his former Chagrin Valley horse show experience, he had been involved in stable setup, the jump crew and nearly every odd job needed to get the horse show up and running.[23]

Although it was a new focus and leadership for the horse show, many traditions continued. For example, the beautiful silver trophies that had been presented for years became awards at the Chagrin Valley PHA Horse Show. The horse show also continued its focus on hunter, jumper and equitation competition, as well as benefitting the young United States Equestrian Team. Prominent supporters of the show, as well as of the beneficiary, read like a who's who of Cleveland society and included Cyrus Eaton, Mr. and Mrs. George M. Humphrey, Courtney Burton, J. Basil Ward and Mr. and Mrs. Raymond Firestone.

Mapes wrote in his greeting in the 1965 souvenir program:

> *Presenting a successful Horse Show is a difficult job in itself, and trying to follow the sixteen years of success of the Chagrin Valley Trails and Riding Club is like the vaudeville performer following Jack Benny! Through the efforts of the Chagrin Valley Trails & Riding Club, C.P. Wright, President, this show had become one of America's greatest outdoor horse shows—it is that AGAIN this year through the cooperation of many people.*[24]

The show committee was open-minded and full of energy. In 1965, the competition was held on July 22–25 and hosted about four hundred horses and ponies from fifteen states during its four-day schedule of fifty-three classes that ended with the nation's first grand prix show jumping event. More than twenty thousand spectators were in attendance for the hunter and jumper classes. All of the divisions were extremely well filled, and the Junior Hunter Division had more than eighty-five entries. The winner of the Division A Championship 13 and Under was a horse named Miltown, shown by Katie Monahan. Mary Jane Chapman's Citadel won the 14–17 years Division B Championship.

Rodney Jenkins, with Jazztime, accepts a hunter championship from Chairman Chuck Mapes. *Chagrin Valley PHA Horse Shows Inc.*

Other hunter honors went to George Jayne's Radar, ridden to Working Hunter Championship by Ruth Engel. First Year Green Working Champion was Copyright, ridden by Bunny Kizorek, and Second Year Green Champion was Michele Jacob's Medalia S, ridden by Chuck Graham.

In the Conformation Hunter Division, Felix Nuesch's Jazztime was shown to the tricolor by Rodney Jenkins, and Debra Wilson's Rome Dome was Green Conformation champ. The Amateur-Owner Hunter Division was won by Mrs. G.E. Little's Sungirt. Pam Carmichael's Gay Minstrel won the Pony Hunter Championship.

Jumper entries also increased in 1965, and Mary Mairs Chapot dominated the Open Division aboard her Anakonda. The Green Jumper Championship went to Glefke's Hunt and Hack entry, Red Yount, ridden by Rodney Jenkins. Dorchester Farms' local entry Double Trouble, ridden by Ken Kraus, won the Junior Jumper Championship.

A sudden windstorm disrupted the show on Saturday afternoon, halting the Open Jumper Stake for an hour after the fences were flattened. After the course was rebuilt, the class continued, but perhaps that telling incident was a premonition of Mother Nature's interest in future horse shows.[25]

Chapter 4

NATIONAL INFLUENCES ON THE LOCAL EQUESTRIAN SCENE

A number of changes in the national and international horse world impacted and inspired the activities and evolution of show jumping in the Chagrin Valley.

Originally, horse shows were independent local events run under their own rules. In 1917, a move was made to unite the independent shows under a single governing body for the United States, organized as the American Horse Shows Association (AHSA). Representatives of fifty horse shows under the leadership of Reginald C. Vanderbilt met in New York City to unify horsemen and women from the North, South, East and West and establish parameters for clean, fair competition in the show ring. By 1919, the AHSA listed thirty-five member shows in the United States. However, shows in Cleveland and Chagrin Valley did not become members until later.

The focus of the AHSA was governing only American shows because international teams were overseen by the military. In 1935, the AHSA appointed a committee to explore joining the International Equestrian Federation (FEI). The committee, subject to the agreement of the Cavalry Association, recommended that after the 1936 Olympic games, the AHSA take over the United States membership in the FEI, which agreed that its rules applied only to the international military classes.

From the first Olympic equestrian competition in 1912 until 1948, the Olympic and international rules required that all equestrian competitors from all countries be active-duty members of the military. The Olympic and National teams from 1912 through 1948 were composed entirely of active-duty army officers and horses that often competed in multiple disciplines on teams for show jumping, dressage and three-day eventing.

Fred Klink of the U.S. Cavalry Association shared his early memories with the author. Today, the Olympic disciplines have dedicated teams that specialize in show jumping (over a course of obstacles), dressage (performing predetermined patterns of precision maneuvers) or three-day eventing (a triathlon of stadium jumping, dressage and cross-country jumping). In the early games, American teams were primarily focused on show jumping. Although the 1912 Olympic team that traveled to Stockholm had no experience competing in dressage or three-day eventing, the team still won a silver medal in three-day eventing.

According to Klink, jumping was different in those days. The courses tended to be circular with only one or two changes of direction. Jumping was scored differently as well; faults were awarded for touching a rail even if it didn't fall down. It was permissible to stop and/or walk to a starting point that you considered optimum for approaching a given jump. The U.S. Army's cavalry headquarters at Fort Riley, Kansas, was the center of the universe as far as American equestrian competition was concerned, and nearly all the cavalry Olympic teams trained there, explained Klink.

Major Louis A. DiMarco wrote in "The Army Equestrian Olympic Team":

> *Although the official participation of the Army ended after the 1948 Games, the Army continued to be a key factor in U.S. equestrian Olympic sport through the interest and expertise of its veteran horsemen. To compete in the Olympic games with a civilian team the U.S. had to create a civilian equestrian organization. This organization eventually became the U.S. Equestrian Team (USET), charged with organizing, training and administering U.S. teams in international equestrian competition. The first president of USET was Colonel John Wofford, a retired cavalryman who was a member of the 1932 Olympic team and horsemanship instructor at Fort Riley. Beginning in its formative years and continuing through the early 1960s, Army officers were critical to running, maintaining and improving the USET. Retired generals Frederick Wing, Tupper Cole, and Fred Boye played key roles. General Cole, among other things, was the Chef d'Equipe for the 1956 USET. Virtually all the Olympic veterans operated behind the scenes organizing and judging local competitions, assisting with administration, and training young horseman.*
>
> *To ensure the first civilian team was well prepared, the Army itself also became involved. For the 1952 Games the Army lent the Fort Riley*

John Russell (shown here on Rattler) rode in the 1952 Olympic games on the first "civilian" U.S. Equestrian Team. *Show Jumping Hall of Fame.*

facilities to USET and leased veteran Army horses to the team for a dollar. Democrat, the horse on which Colonel Franklin Wing almost won a silver jumping medal in 1948, was one of the one-dollar Army horses. Nineteen years old in 1952, Democrat became Major John Russell's mount and contributed to the Bronze Medal achievement of the 1952 jumping team.[26]

When selection trials were held for the first-ever civilian U.S. Equestrian Team at Fort Riley in 1951, Carol Hagerman Durand became the first female rider to qualify for an Olympic team. She was widely considered to have been America's leading lady rider in the immediate post–World War II era. The International Olympic Committee (IOC) eventually sustained its exclusion of female show jumpers for the 1952 Olympics, and four years later, the IOC changed its posture on female riding. The squad at the 1952 Helsinki games included Arthur McCashin, who rode Miss Budweiser, a horse Carol Durand had been showing in the American shows. The third member of that first civilian show jumping team that earned the bronze medal was William Steinkraus aboard Hollandia.

William Steinkraus recalled:

> *When civilian show-jumpers took over our country's international representation following the cavalry's withdrawal after the 1948 Olympics, they faced a very serious challenge. As our sole official international representatives, our cavalry officers had long been accustomed to competing under international rules over international-type courses, while the civilians' experience had been confined to our very different national rules and courses. Trying to understand a completely unfamiliar set of competitive conditions and adjust to them in just two years was the daunting task that faced the infant USET in 1950. European outdoor courses were (and are) relatively long and complex, using a very wide variety of obstacles including ditches, water and banks. Many obstacles were wide as well as high, and typically only knockdowns and disobediences were scored, within a time limit. The major competition was called the grand prix. American courses, in contrast, were relatively short and simple, built within an enclosed ring with no natural obstacles. Except for one class (the knockdown and out), touches were scored as well as knockdowns, which limited height. (Such simple conditions are still sometimes used for young horses and children.) Time and spread fences were rarely a factor, and the major class was named the Stake (Sweepstake) Class. Standards were high, but it was a different game. Quite a contrast!*
>
> *Success in making the transition from one of these to the other was not immediate, but it is a testament to the determination of our horse community that we made the Olympic podium in 1952 and within a decade became a major factor in the international sport, and from time to time even a dominant one. Though initially we were obliged to train mostly abroad, our domestic rules gradually changed to accommodate spread fences, speed, knockdowns only, natural obstacles and other more European-style variants.*

It wasn't until 1964 at the Tokyo Olympics that the United States show jumping team included female riders, Mary Mairs aboard Tomboy and Kathy Kusner aboard Untouchable. Along with teammate Frank Chapot on San Lucas, they earned a sixth-place team finish.

Americans were proud of their international teams, and that patriotism fueled support of the new United States Equestrian Team among equestrians in the Chagrin Valley. It became a tradition of the Chagrin Valley Trails

1965 Chagrin Valley PHA Horse Show program. *Chagrin Valley PHA Horse Shows Inc.*

and Riding Club Horse Show and its successor, the Chagrin Valley PHA Horse Show, to make USET the beneficiary. Committees raised funds and awareness for the organization to show their support.

Part II

THE CLEVELAND
GRAND PRIX

Chapter 5

THE BIRTH OF THE NATION'S FIRST SHOW JUMPING GRAND PRIX

By presenting the very first truly European-style outdoor show-jumping grand prix in Cleveland in 1965, the organizers played a critical role in the development of our domestic show-jumping sport, and that eventually led to our staging a highly successful complete Olympic equestrian program at Los Angeles in 1984 and the first of several successful World Cup Finals at Baltimore in 1980. Now, almost a half century later, it is no longer essential for us to go to Europe to experience European show-jumping conditions, and leading international riders from around the world routinely compete against our homegrown riders in major grands prix in this country. All this certainly wasn't accomplished either effortlessly or overnight, but our equestrian community can take great pride in the progress we have achieved since 1965 and the splendid international records our riders have chalked up.
—William Steinkraus, Show Jumping Hall of Fame inductee, five-time Olympian and first American to win an individual equestrian gold medal in Show Jumping

If you visit the Cleveland Metroparks Polo Field today, you will see a bronze Ohio Historical Marker that recognizes the significance of the Cleveland Grand Prix with brief text, but there is so much more to the story.

The concept of a grand prix jumping competition in the United States began to evolve after Hungarian immigrant Laddie Andahazy's interest was piqued by the German Equestrian Team's clean sweep during the 1936 Olympics. "I dreamed of having an equestrian exhibition such as what I saw in Europe," he said. In the 1960s, Andahazy was director of Riding at

Lake Erie College and visited equestrian centers on behalf of the college's Academic Term Abroad program. During his travels, he collected literature and photographs. He also brought back a small show jumping handbook that detailed fence construction and diagrams of European course designs, including the 1936 Olympic course.[27] "When I traveled to Italy, Germany and France, I visited as many equestrian areas as I could. I wanted to transfer what I saw. When I made a presentation at the Chagrin Valley Hunt Club and showed the films and slides I had collected, everyone was very interested," said Andahazy.[28]

Among those who were interested was D. Jerry Baker. Baker had competed successfully with the U.S. Army Team and in the 1960s was general manager and trainer for J. Basil Ward's Hound's Hill Stables in Gates Mills, Ohio. Baker approached Chuck Mapes and Leah Goetz (Stroud) at the Blue Lakes Farm horse show in Newbury, Ohio, about holding a grand prix and stated that he thought he could get the backing of Mr. Ward. "I told them that I wanted to give $3,000 away, and they thought I had taken leave of my senses. They didn't really know where I was going to come up with the money, and I said that if they'd let me do it, I would be sure that I would come up with the money," said Baker.[29]

"Jerry Baker mentioned to Basil Ward that we should try to finance a big jumping exhibition on the polo field similar to what I had seen in Europe. Jerry was the one who got Mr. Ward to put up $3,000 for a big event. That was going to be the first grand prix," added Andahazy.[30]

In 1965, Baker headed the new Grand Prix Committee of the Chagrin Valley PHA Horse Show. In addition to Andahazy, other members of the Grand Prix Committee who organized the class included Esther L. Voorhees, Leah Goetz, Edward T. Clark, Raymond Francis, Herbert Lilly, Charles E. Mapes, Jerome Rogers and Donald Snellings.[31]

The sunny Sunday afternoon of July 25, 1965, brought a new era to show jumping in North America. A field of twenty-nine horses piloted by twenty riders competed in the first North American show jumping grand prix—the Cleveland Grand Prix. Flags from six countries—the United States, Canada, Mexico, France, Great Britain and Germany—flew at the first Cleveland Grand Prix. Although thirty-five horses had been nominated earlier in the week, only twenty-nine made it to the big event held on the Cleveland Metroparks Polo Field.

Dr. Paul Weaver, president of Lake Erie College, acted as master of ceremonies and welcomed visiting dignitaries from the Professional Horseman's Association, American Horse Shows Association and United

Local trainer Don Snellings, pictured here at Dorchester Farms on Anthony A, was among the first Cleveland Grand Prix entries. *Chagrin Valley PHA Horse Shows Inc.*

States Equestrian Team. The advance festivities included the U.S. Marine Corps Color Guard and a thrilling dressage exhibition performed by Donna Sharp Plumb aboard the famed eleven-year-old Attache. Cleveland Mounted Police led a parade of riders onto the field while an organ played the six national anthems. A bell called the first horse to the field, and Dr. Weaver introduced each entry as they entered the competition arena and prepared to face the course. Herr Richard Watjen, reportedly the oldest active horse master of world fame, accepted the salute of the grand prix riders.[32]

The Cleveland Grand Prix Course

The Cleveland Grand Prix was defined by the 844-yard course of sixteen obstacles and a total of three rounds, including the jump-off. By today's standards, the course path was very straightforward, the kind of track you

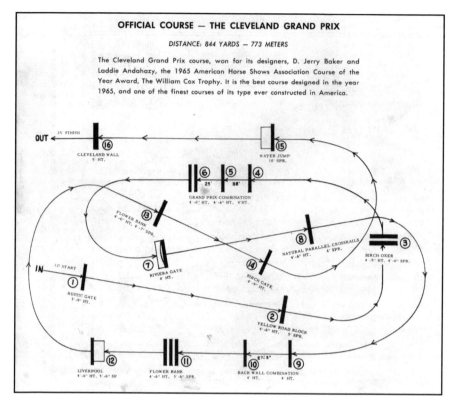

The first Cleveland Grand Prix course design by Laddie Andahazy and D. Jerry Baker. *Chagrin Valley PHA Horse Shows Inc.*

would see in a hunter ring with long lines and only two changes of direction. However, it was like nothing the U.S. competitors—or spectators—had ever seen before. The course earned the team of Baker and Andahazy the 1965 American Horse Shows Association Course of the Year Award.

The Cleveland course was modified from the European courses Andahazy had seen. In Europe, water jumps were sixteen feet, and in Cleveland, the water jump for the first grand prix was ten feet. The water jump was considered the most hazardous because of its width. The fences were very intimidating individually and collectively as a course of obstacles to be tackled in succession. For example, the last fence of the Cleveland Grand Prix was the Cleveland Wall, a simulated white stone wall of graduated sectional blocks with pillars on the sides.

Noted U.S. Equestrian Team dignitaries who attended the event included USET captain William Steinkraus, coach Bert de Nemethy and president

Judging the water jump. *Chagrin Valley PHA Horse Shows Inc.*

Whitney Stone. They watched carefully, knowing that the future of U.S. representation in international competition depended on better show jumping opportunities at home.

Olympic medal winner Steinkraus was quoted in the media as saying the course "represents the only one in the U.S. which is as challenging and as beautiful as those we have seen in Europe, England and Japan."[33]

The First Cleveland Grand Prix

More than ten thousand people were on hand to witness the first grand prix and caught a glimpse of a multimillion-dollar sport in the making. The roster of male and female riders included such noted equestrians as Canadian Jim Day, Rodney Jenkins, Sonny Brooks (the first African American show jumping rider), Max Bonham and the husband-and-wife team of Mary and Frank Chapot, who represented the United States Equestrian Team.

Only Mary and Frank Chapot were experienced in jumping a course of that caliber, due to their experience riding on the U.S. Equestrian Team. According to Chuck Kinney, who served on the jump crew, the jump order was altered from the customary random draw so that Mary Chapot would go first in the class. He said organizers reasoned that if the other riders saw a lady jump around successfully it would encourage others and keep them from "chickening out" of jumping the imposing course.

In order to be eligible to compete in the grand prix, horses had to be shown in two other classes during the Chagrin Valley PHA Horse Show and pay an entry fee of $100. The grand prix comprised two rounds of competition and a tie-breaking jump-off, if necessary. Among the officials

Spectators in the VIP seats. *Chagrin Valley PHA Horse Shows Inc.*

The first Cleveland Grand Prix pair on course was Mary Chapot and Tomboy. *Photo by Marshall P. Hawkins Photo, courtesy of Robert McClanahan.*

scoring faults that day sat honorary judge Kathy Kusner, a member of the U.S. Olympic team the year before in Tokyo.

First to go on course, Mary Chapot rode her mare, Tomboy. The pair jumped around in good form and made it look easy, riding forward and jumping faultlessly. *The Chronicle of the Horse* described their historic round:

> *Tomboy started over the first three fences with extreme ease. Then came the first combination of the Grand Prix. Riders gathered to the sidelines to witness the distance as Tomboy made the first fence very well, taking two rather long strides to the second fence, over easily, one very long stride and over the double oxer, with no apparent difficulty. She turned, jumped the 7th and 8th fences, and made a sweeping right-hand turn to negotiate the second combination along the back wall of the course, two very large vertical fences. The third fence of that line, not part of the combination, was rather demanding to ride to. Tomboy started forward, and it proved just difficult enough, for her rider had to take back and then drive forward*

again. Jumping it well, she went straight on to a rather large liverpool. Taking another rather long right turn, Tomboy faced the first five-foot flower oxer which she met in complete full stride, left the ground easily and continued to a very large birch gate. Again, jumping with no difficulty, and to this time with no faults, she made her left turn to face the 16-foot water jump—actually 10 feet of water but requiring a 16-foot spread to clear it. Mary, riding in excellent form, never took back, but drove the big chestnut forward; they met the water jump perfectly, were clean, and continued over a 5-foot stone wall without fault.[34]

Chapot was one of several female riders to compete that day. In addition to Tomboy, she rode Anakonda in the grand prix and was the only woman to finish with a clean round. Other female competitors included Laura Nichols on her Gun Club and Great Idea, Ruth Engel on Wildcat for C. Schott and George Jayne, Bunny Kizorek on S. Jayne's Fair Trade and Betty Oare (entered as Mrs. E.M. Oare), who rode her hunter Navy Commander.

Oare recalled the following during an interview with the author:

Navy Commander was the Working Hunter Champion of the country, and he had never done anything like the grand prix. He was so brave…it was a real thrill. He only had one rail that he rolled, and it was my fault. I remember riding in the parade before the grand prix with Rodney Jenkins—we were friends from Virginia, and he was riding Blue Plum, who was owned by the Firestones. I still have that picture of the parade. We were allowed to take a piece of greenery home, and my dad took home a bush that is still in my backyard. Ernie and I had only been married a year at that time, and I entered as Mrs. E.M. Oare and was happy to be. All our lives we have entered our horses as Mr. and Mrs. E.M. Oare. This is one sport where women are equally as strong as men, especially in the jumpers. I never thought about men versus women—I just wanted to make the horse go well.

During the grand prix, Max Bonham was injured in the first round of competition; he had the only serious fall on course, ironically aboard J. Basil Ward's horse, Emmie K. After a trip to the hospital for a check-over, he returned to the show grounds to see the conclusion of the event from the sidelines.

After the first round of competition, eight riders proceeded to the next round or first jump-off, which produced three fault-free rounds. The final tie-breaking jump-off was held over a grueling course of eight fences ranging in

Honorary judge Kathy Kusner shown aboard Aberali. *Chagrin Valley PHA Horse Shows Inc.*

height from five feet to the ominous six-foot-two-inch Cleveland Wall. Time determined the results of the second jump-off. Mary Chapot went first in the tie-breaking jump-off and had a fast time of 51.5 seconds with eight faults for knocking down the wall and faulting at the liverpool (for stepping in the water portion of the jump). Frank Chapot, veteran of three Olympic games, followed her round and also had eight faults but a slower time of 56.8 seconds aboard Manon, a French-bred mare. The final challenger, Rodney Jenkins and Sure Thing, had trouble with a refusal and knockdown, which left them with fifteen faults and the third-place ribbon.[35]

Frank Chapot's other mount, Good Twist, finished fourth with four faults after round two. Prior to the grand prix, Sonny Brooks of New Jersey had bailed off a falling horse during a qualifying class. He was able to complete the qualifying round riding another horse, but he rode with a broken arm above the wrist and waited to go to the hospital after he was done qualifying for the grand prix. Brooks rode The Imp in the grand prix with his arm in a cast and finished fifth, with four faults over the two rounds.

Canadian Jim Day, aboard the famous jumper Nanticoke, finished in sixth place over the inaugural course with a two-round score of eight faults. They were followed in the ribbons by Rodney Jenkins and his other mount, Blue Plum.

There were many accomplishments that day, but it was Mary Chapot who bested the show jumping competitors aboard her chestnut mare, Tomboy, to take home the $1,200 winner's share of the $3,000 purse. She also received a twenty-inch silver trophy donated by Ward, president of Addressograph Multigraph, and a blanket of red carnations (the Ohio state flower) and a red, white and blue blanket-cooler.

1965 Cleveland Grand Prix Results

Place	Horse	Rider	Owner	Score	Prize Money
1	Tomboy	Mary Mairs Chapot	Cheeca Farm	0-0-8/51.5	$1,200
2	Manon	Frank Chapot	Cheeca Farm	0-0-8/56.8	$650
3	Sure Thing	Rodney Jenkins	Chance Hill Farm	0-0-15/66.6	$450
4	Good Twist	Frank Chapot	Cheeca Farm	0-4	$300
5	The Imp	Sonny Brooks	A.B.S. Farm	0-4	$200
6	Nanticoke	Jim Day	Fairfield Farm	0-8	$100
7	Blue Plum	Rodney Jenkins	Chance Hill Farm	0-12	$50
8	Grey Aero	Frank Imperator	Frank Imperator	0-E	$50

Following the grand prix, the participants relaxed at Mr. and Mrs. Gilbert Humphrey's nearby residence, Hunting Hill, before heading home.

From an early age, Mary Chapot had built a record of equestrian accomplishments. In 1960, she won the ASPCA Maclay and AHSA Medal Championships, which are judged on equitation, or the rider's physical style and mental ability to negotiate a course. She was the first woman and still one of only a few riders to accomplish both these wins. One year later, at the age of seventeen, she became the youngest female rider for the United States Equestrian Team. Two years before the Cleveland Grand Prix, Mary Chapot struck gold with Tomboy, winning the team and individual gold medals at the 1963 Pan American Games in Brazil. The year before Cleveland, the pair made their Olympic debut at the 1964 Tokyo games. During an interview with the author, Chapot recalled:

When I rode at Cleveland, we didn't know what grand prix were at that time, and it was very special. The course was beautifully decorated with flowers and was longer than any course we had ever seen before...Tomboy was a Thoroughbred by Wait A Bit, out of Jane Tana, a mare that Show Jumping Hall of Fame member Adolph Mogavero showed years earlier. She was of average height and solidly built. You wouldn't have picked her out of a lineup as the Thoroughbred in the group. She had an easy temperament and was pretty laid back to ride. Bert de Nemethy always worried about her fitness, so we were often sent to the upper field at Gladstone for a gallop. In the barn, she was easy to deal with other than the usual ears back at feeding time. When I met her, she was a green jumper with Dave Kelley. I tried her out as a possibility to ride in the Medal and Maclay Finals, then in New York. That wasn't going to work, but I loved her, and my parents bought her for me that fall. We trained briefly with Jimmy Williams in California before being selected for further training from the USET Screening Trials. We went on to ride with the U.S. Team, training with Bert de Nemethy and, of course, my husband, Frank Chapot. She wasn't the fastest—probably because I didn't know what I was doing—and she probably couldn't jump as high as some, but she was very, very consistent, jumping many clear rounds in Nations Cups.

After winning that first grand prix in Cleveland, Mary Chapot and Tomboy went on to win several more big classes, including the prestigious John Player Trophy in London. At the 1967 Pan American Games in Winnipeg, Canada, the pair earned a silver medal, and in the 1968

Awards presentation with Mrs. Gilbert Humphrey and J. Basil Ward. *Chagrin Valley PHA Horse Shows Inc.*

Olympic games in Mexico City, she and her teammates rode to a fourth-place finish.

After retiring from international competition Chapot went on to coach her daughters, Wendy and Laura, who both had much success competing on the horse show circuit. Tomboy eventually retired with an injury and had one foal, a stallion called Good News Joe, who sired several good horses.

In 1977, Baker reflected on the first Cleveland Grand Prix during a local interview with WBKC Radio:

> *The country needed the change, or the sport was going to go right down the drain. It was a gamble, but it was a gamble that paid off. Naturally, there were mistakes made. I'd made mistakes in designing the course—not drastic mistakes, but things that had to be corrected. Nevertheless, we got show jumping off the ground in Cleveland...I remember in 1965 the first year that we held it, there were two members of the U.S. Equestrian Team there, and they came up to me after they walked the course and said, "Jerry, do*

you realize that this is longer than the Grand Prix of Aachen (Germany) and it's bigger?" I said, "Yes." And then I said, "Do you realize that this is the Grand Prix of Cleveland?" And with that they turned around and walked away. I'm happy to say they won it. Bert de Nemethy was there—he backed it completely. It was that sort of day, that sort of an event. And it was at the right time. The country needed a change, and as I look over my career, I'm glad I was part of the change.[36]

Chapter 6

THE 1960s:
THE SOARING, SOAKING '60s

Everybody wants to win the event in Cleveland. There are a lot of horse races—there's only one Kentucky Derby. There's a lot of grand prix—there's only one Cleveland. When I do the course, I do it with that in mind. I try to build a very demanding course.
—D. Jerry Baker[37]

After its incredible Cleveland Grand Prix debut in 1965, the Chagrin Valley PHA Board proved it wasn't a one-hit wonder and continued to host large audiences to see the best equestrians. Through the second half of the 1960s, the entries in the Cleveland Grand Prix continued to grow, as did the number of spectators and fans of the sport.

During the 1960s, the horse show world took notice of the popular Cleveland Grand Prix format and studied the results. If imitation is the greatest form of flattery, then Cleveland had reached a pinnacle, as horse shows across America began adding their own grand prix to their schedules in the years following the important debut.

In 1966, Carlene Blunt of Del Ray Beach, Florida, won the second Cleveland Grand Prix aboard her horse Silver Lining. Following a major rainstorm that left the grass field soaked, forty-three horses galloped onto the course for the first round. Eight returned for the jump-off. Silver Lining, appropriately named for the post-storm victory, emerged the winner after the second jump-off.

An aerial view of the show grounds at the Cleveland Metroparks Polo Field, 1966. *Chagrin Valley PHA Horse Shows Inc.*

The 1966 award ceremony with Carlene Blunt, Mrs. Raymond Firestone and J. Basil Ward. *Chagrin Valley PHA Horse Shows Inc.*

The ringmaster announces the start of the competition. *Chagrin Valley PHA Horse Shows Inc.*

Blunt reflected years later:

> *Winning the Cleveland Grand Prix in 1966 was very special for me and my wonderful horse Silver Lining...I had never seen such a beautiful course. The jumps were big but so beautiful that you really wanted to jump them. I think the flower bank was the most beautiful. It was very wide but so inviting that the horses jumped it very well—it was really a fun course. It was a memorable day also because when we were all lined up and ready for the parade, band and all, the heavens opened up, sending everyone back to the barns in a hurry. It was doubtful the class would be able to take place, but a few hours later, the rain was over and the class was held. The Cleveland Grand Prix was very instrumental in the success that grand prix jumping is enjoying in this country today.*[38]

The day after the 1966 Cleveland Grand Prix, the horse show held the Team Competition class for the American Horse Shows Association Zone

5 Junior Jumper Championship. Organizers provided a unique opportunity for the young riders to compete over a lowered Cleveland Grand Prix course, still set from the prior day. Among those junior riders who went on to become professionals were Steve Stephens, Dennis Mitchell, Susie Schoellkopf and Clevelanders Ken Kraus and Karen Jackson (Schneider).

The already daunting Cleveland Grand Prix became an even greater challenge. Several new obstacles were permanently built into the course for the 1967 event, including a new liverpool or water jump surrounded by shrubs, and the existing water jump was enlarged to twelve feet. That year also saw a new addition: a double bank jump. It was built by Jerry Osborne of the Osborne Construction Company, a member of the Grand Prix Committee, at a cost of about $5,000.[39]

Rodney Jenkins could have been named king of the horse show in 1967, as he carried home the lion's share of awards for jumper divisions during the week, as well as the Cleveland Grand Prix. He rode five excellent horses in the big class, including Nanticoke and Blue Plum, who was the Open Jumper division champion. Unfortunately, those two horses had bad luck in the first round of the Cleveland Grand Prix and were eliminated. It was the lightly shown Harry Gill entry of Gustavus that emerged victorious at the end of a third round between Jenkins and Canada's Doug Henry, in his first U.S. show aboard Beacon Hill. Young rider Meg Woodington and Strike Up qualified for the third round but withdrew in fatigue, happy to take home third place.[40]

Canadians Take Cleveland by Storm

The Cleveland Grand Prix was recognized in North America for its difficulty and ability to single out the finest jumpers. In 1968, the Canadian Equestrian Team used the event as a basis for final team selections for the Mexico City Olympics, and the Canadian Broadcasting System televised the class.

The Cleveland Grand Prix that year was the largest course in the nation, with the Cleveland Wall reaching six feet, six inches in height. Sixty horses entered, but only thirty-eight started, and among them there were six rider falls during the three rounds. The Canadians performed superbly. Six of their eight horses jumped clean in the first round, while former Grand Prix winners Silver Lining and Gustavus did not. Canadian Jim Day rode Ernest Samuel's bright chestnut Canadian Club to win the big event with twenty thousand spectators cheering and the Canadian

The challenging course took its toll on inexperienced horses and riders. *Courtesy of Chagrin Valley PHA Horse Shows Inc.*

1968 Cleveland Grand Prix winner Canadian Club and Canada's Jim Day. *Chagrin Valley PHA Horse Shows Inc.*

The 1968 award ceremony with Mr. and Mrs. George M. Humphrey (right) and Mr. and Mrs. Raymond Firestone (left). *Chagrin Valley PHA Horse Shows Inc.*

selection committee watching from the VIP seats. Fellow Canadian Terrance Miller rode Beefeater to second place with a time of 1:02, slower than Day's 47.74-second time. Jim Day went on to Mexico and rode on the gold medal Olympic Team for Canada.[41]

It was a tradition to honor special guests during the Cleveland Grand Prix, and in 1968, the committee honored horseman George M. Humphrey, former Secretary of the Treasury under President Dwight Eisenhower. Humphrey, of Gates Mills, was also the former Master of Fox Hounds of the Chagrin Valley Hunt. Most of his family was present for the grand prix, including his granddaughter Margo, who was married to Canadian Team member J. Moffat Dunlap. Following the grand prix, the gracious Humphreys hosted a supper for the team.[42]

The big story in 1969 was the weather, as it continued to plague the horse show. The same weather pattern had drenched the Oak Brook, Illinois horse show to the west of Cleveland the prior week and forced the cancellation of its grand prix. Unfortunately, as competitors left one devastating storm, they headed east with the weather, not realizing that flooding from the rains had caused the Chagrin River to drown the Cleveland Metroparks Polo Field show grounds in five feet of water. On

Left: The weather took its toll on the show in 1969. *Chagrin Valley PHA Horse Shows Inc.*

Below: Jerry Baker assesses water and wind damage. *Chagrin Valley PHA Horse Shows Inc.*

Sunday, a caravan of horse trailers driving from Illinois parked any place they could along the highway, as there was no place for them to go until the flooding drained. In the end, however, the show went on.[43]

The Cleveland Grand Prix proved successful for Canada once again, as J. Moffat Dunlap returned to win aboard the big black gelding Lights Out and become the second Canadian winner in a row. Lights Out turned in two clean rounds to secure the win, and there was a three-way tie between the seasoned four-faulters for second place. The tie included the 1968 winners Canadian Club and Jim Day, 1966 winners Silver Lining and Carlene Blunt and U.S. Olympian Kathy Kusner riding Aberali, who had been purchased from the Italian Olympic Team by USET supporters Mr. and Mrs. Patrick Butler.[44]

Kusner, known as the best female rider in the world, showed her amazing talent and courage that day. Early in the grand prix, she rode another mount, That's Right, who crashed through a fence, unseating Kusner in a dramatic fall, kicking her in the head and knocking her unconscious. Riding with a mild concussion, she finished the grand prix on her other horse, Sunshine, and rode Aberali in the second round. Later in her career, Kusner traded her riding coat for jockey silks and took the racing world by storm.

The 1969 course was made even more difficult by the addition of another new jump, Pulvermann's Grab (*grab* is German for "grave"), named for Germany's Major Fritz Pulvermann, the designer who would be killed jumping it in Germany a year later. Adding to the difficulty in the Chagrin Valley that year, riders were challenged by a particularly deep and sloppy course, flooded by the rain that stopped the horse show for two days. Despite the weather conditions, thirteen thousand fans turned out to witness the efforts of the competitors. Although Canada claimed the Cleveland Grand Prix, Mother Nature proved her strength over the horse show.

Chapter 7

THE 1970s:
GROWTH, INNOVATION AND
A SPINOFF

B y the 1970s, horse shows across America were continuing to add grand
prix to their schedules. Cleveland was still the grand prix to watch, and
the Chagrin Valley PHA Horse Show had earned a well-deserved reputation
for innovation.

The horse show committee continued to host the best grand prix in the
nation, and up-and-coming young riders who wanted to make a name for
themselves knew Cleveland was their stage. In 1970, twenty-year-old Steve
Stephens of Palmetto, Florida, expanded his show jumping résumé by
winning the $5,000 Cleveland Grand Prix aboard Mrs. R.J. Reynolds's Toy
Soldier. Stephens was coached to the winner's circle by his trainer, former
Clevelander Eugene Mische, who had moved to Florida to start his business
in the 1960s.

One ongoing requirement for competing in the Cleveland Grand Prix was
for the horses to show in a jumper class during the week prior to the event.
This practice gave fans a preview of the competition, allowing them to scout
their favorite horses and riders. It also built overall spectator attendance and
excitement leading up to the grand prix, as well as an educated audience. In

Opposite, top: 1970 Cleveland Grand Prix winner Steve Stephens, shown here going over the
fourteen-foot water jump on Mighty Ruler and wearing the leading rider sash. *Chagrin Valley
PHA Horse Shows Inc.*

Opposite, bottom: Harry de Leyer and Dutch Brandy jumping off the Osborne Bank. *Chagrin
Valley PHA Horse Shows Inc.*

1970, a popular grand prix crowd favorite was the veteran rider Harry de Leyer aboard Dutch Brandy. The Long Island, New York father of eight had a near-spill on course at the Osborne Bank and rode under his horse's neck until he recovered before the next obstacle to clear it and thrill the crowd. In addition to earning their admiration, de Leyer claimed the red second-place ribbon that day.

Winning the Cleveland Grand Prix was the biggest moment in Stephens's life at the time. Today, he still says that was his favorite grand prix win. He went on to become one of the top international show jumping course designers and continued to return to the Chagrin Valley over the years to design the Cleveland Grand Prix course.[45]

The American Gold Cup

In 1970, fans were treated to a double-header in Cleveland as they saw the debut of another large-scale show jumping event, the American Gold Cup, which was held Sunday following Saturday's Cleveland Grand Prix. The Gold Cup offered $25,000 in prize money and was a no-fee event, so there was no financial burden on exhibitors. Founded by Cleveland Grand Prix organizer Jerry Baker, the event was originally scheduled for Soldier's Field in Chicago near another Baker show in Oak Brook, Illinois. However, the venue was changed to Cleveland a few months before the inaugural event due to cost concerns in constructing the obstacles in Chicago.

Fans saw European-style show jumping over obstacles that included gates, walls, water jumps, bank jumps and the famous Pulvermann's Grab. The ultimate goal was improving U.S. show jumping for future international competitions, and it was fitting that the horse show committee had named Whitney Stone, president of the U.S. Equestrian Team, the honorary chairman that year.

The winner of the first American Gold Cup in Cleveland was Act One, a nine-year-old bay gelding owned by businessman Michael McEvoy and ridden by Conrad Homfeld, twenty-one, of Lagrangeville, New York. The pair had competed in the Cleveland Grand Prix the day before but had faults in the jump-off and finished fifth. Jumping two major competitions back to back didn't prove too tiring for the pair. In the Gold Cup, Homfeld had four faults in the first round, none in the second and jumped clean and fast in the final jump-off to win. In addition to the $6,000 top prize, their names were first on the PHA's Gold Cup trophy. Act One had competed on the United States Equestrian team in 1968, as well as competed successfully as a junior jumper with McEvoy's daughter, Michele. Rodney Jenkins of Orange, Virginia, aboard Harry Gill's Idle Dice challenged, but an unlucky rail down in the timed jump-off kept them from victory. Crowd-pleaser Harry de Leyer finished third.[46]

After the American Gold Cup was introduced in Cleveland, Baker, who had worked with Gene Mische on the event concept, moved it to Tampa Stadium in Florida. In 1971, Steve Stephens won the $15,000 Gold Cup on his home turf aboard Houdini. The Cleveland spinoff became the first grand prix held in a major outdoor stadium in the United States.

However, the American Gold Cup didn't stay in Tampa any longer than it stayed in Cleveland. Baker nullified a ten-year Tampa contract and moved the Gold Cup again, this time to the Rose Bowl in Pasadena, California. In 1973, his troubles continued when the $200,000 American Gold Cup series, which was scheduled for six West Coast cities, was cancelled a month before it was set to begin with a full roster of international entries. U.S. professionals threatened a class-action suit against Baker, who was under contract to run the series. The American Gold Cup eventually found a home in Devon, Pennsylvania, where it ran for more than three decades.[47] It was replaced in Tampa by another great outdoor event, the American Invitational.

Cleveland Grand Prix

In 1971, the Cleveland Grand Prix was back in the spotlight on Sunday afternoon—the culmination and finale of the ninety-six-class horse show. U.S. Olympian Frank Chapot of New Jersey, who had finished second in the first Cleveland Grand Prix to his wife, Mary, won first prize aboard Sandrellan Stable's Grey Carrier. The July win was an upset over favorites Steve Stephens and Houdini, who had won the April American Gold Cup in Tampa. They were edged out during the third round and finished second. A record crowd nearing sixteen thousand was on hand, and other than a stunning fall resulting in minor injuries for Harry de Leyer, the only upset noted was verbal. Canadian Olympic gold medalist Jim Day withdrew his horses from the grand prix in a protest over the water jump. Course designer Jerry Baker had planned a route that required horses to jump over a huge sixteen-foot water spread then to jump-off the bank jump into water.

"I've been training my horses since 1968 to jump over water, and I'm not about to ask them to jump into water here in Cleveland," 1968 Cleveland Grand Prix winner Jim Day told the media. However, Baker refused to alter the course and said, "The Osborne Bank and the splash that follows have the enthusiastic approval of U.S. Coach Bert de Nemethy."[48] The course continued as planned, with Chapot the victor.

In 1972, the Cleveland Grand Prix saw another first—one with local significance. The grand prix was won by a local horse, and a long shot at that. Rosie Report, a six-year-old grey mare owned by J. Basil Ward and trained by Jerry Baker, was ridden to victory by twenty-one-year-old Michael Matz riding out of Gates Mills. Baker admitted he didn't think the mare had enough experience for the tough course. Matz was one of seven entries to jump clean in the first round aboard the relatively inexperienced horse. The heavy favorites were Act One, the first American Gold Cup winner, and Sympatico, who had won two big jumper classes earlier in the week. Both of those horses were ridden by New York's eighteen-year-old Anthony D'Ambrosio Jr. During the second round, a calm and relaxed Matz and Rosie jumped a clean round to win without an additional jump-off, as all of the other horses had faults. Sympatico, with the fastest four-fault round, finished second, and third place went to nineteen-year-old Katie Monahan, riding Sable Cape for the first time. Monahan was catch-riding for Gay Wiles, who had broken her collarbone in a fall.

The grand prix showcased many talented young riders who went on to international acclaim, including Matz, who was happy to have won the grand prix for Ward, a lifelong horseman since his cavalry days in World War I. "He loved the show, and it made me feel very proud for him," said Matz.[49]

Ward's horses were successful for him in the show ring, but he was most proud of having loaned his jumpers Mighty Ruler and Snow Flurry to the United States Equestrian Team in Europe. When Ward retired from the business world, he dispersed his show stable after the 1973 show season, and Mighty Ruler, who had been ridden by Matz, was sold to his new patron, F. Eugene Dixon. Matz later returned to win the Cleveland Grand Prix in 1981 aboard another Dixon entry, the popular Jet Run. After much show jumping success, including international acclaim as the U.S. Olympic flag-bearer, Matz became successful in the horse racing world, training such stars as Barbaro.

Behind the Scenes

As the Chagrin Valley PHA Horse Show and Cleveland Grand Prix grew in popularity, horse show entries soared to nine hundred in 1972. However, growth also presented problems because with nearly one hundred classes, the horse show schedule needed to run tightly or run out of light at the end of a long day. The volunteer officers were diligent about seeing that things ran like clockwork. Behind-the-scenes details such as water and electric supply, stabling and grounds space were addressed by stable manager Chuck Kinney, who faced major growing pains.

Transforming the Cleveland Metroparks Polo Field into a top national horse show facility was no small feat. Approximately 130,000 square feet of tenting was erected to stable the entries. Constructing the show from the ground up required considerable manpower, and crews of high school and college students from the Chagrin Valley assisted over three weeks and came back for another two weeks after the event to dismantle the grounds. Each horse stabled on the grounds during the week required an average of seventeen gallons of

The 1972 show grounds with grand prix course in foreground and stable tents in the background. *Chagrin Valley PHA Horse Shows Inc.*

water for drinking and thirteen gallons for grooming purposes per day. The stable committee supplemented the existing water supply with special pump systems installed in the Chagrin River just for the show.

Traffic control prior to grand prix Sunday required coordination of the Metropolitan Park Police and police departments from surrounding Chagrin Valley communities, including Shaker Heights, Moreland Hills, Chagrin Falls, Hunting Valley, Orange, Pepper Pike and Bentleyville.

During the 1970s, Stanley Stone Jr., marketing director of the Higbee Company, led the officers of the Chagrin Valley PHA Horse Show as chairman. The vice-chairmen who served during the busy growth years were John Davenport, Walter Furlong, Leah Stroud and treasurer John Forbes. Later, the board members were joined by Vice-Chairmen R. Preston Nash Jr., Charles Kinney Jr. and Howard Lewis. Late in the 1970s, Chairman Stone began sharing his responsibilities with a co-chairman, Leah Stroud.

The board met an average of once a month during the year and maintained an office in Chagrin Falls on Bell Street for show secretaries to operate a month and a half before the show. Because of the size of the show, there was considerable planning and paperwork to create the schedule and conform to American Horse Shows Association (AHSA) standards, which changed annually. The week of the show, the office moved to a trailer on the show grounds, returning to its Chagrin Falls office for two weeks after the show concluded to close the books and make detailed reports to the AHSA.

Minutes of the Chagrin Valley PHA Board of Trustees meetings in 1973 reported a few issues with the permanent obstacles on the grand prix course. The Cleveland Metroparks Polo Field was public domain as part of the park system, and weekend riders were using the Osborne Bank and wearing it down, which the board was concerned would render it unusable. Also, the privet hedge around Pulvermann's Grab was frozen during winter and needed to be replaced. Ironically, after all the water had flooded the show, there was an ongoing problem with a lack of water on the grounds. Also that year, they had 740 stalls ordered but 855 stall reservations. The minutes stated, "The show is just too large for us to handle comfortably. It should go back to a smaller show next year."

Two divisions in particular soared, with entries reaching 160 green hunters and 150 junior riders—a hint at the growth the sport would be experiencing in the future with that many up-and-coming horses and riders eighteen years of age and under competing at the elite level. Also important to the board was the quality of the entries—more than thirty-five horses had earned national championships, and grand prix entries included the all-time leading money-winning jumper Idle Dice, ridden by Rodney Jenkins, as well as industrialist Patrick Butler's Olympic silver medal winner, Sloopy, ridden by Joe Fargis. There were more than sixty horses nominated for the Cleveland Grand Prix that year.

Behind the scenes, the trustees also expressed concerns over maintaining control of the Cleveland Grand Prix, which was overseen by Jerry Baker. They named additional Grand Prix Committee chairmen to oversee the event alongside Baker, who had been responsible for both bringing the American Gold Cup to Cleveland and relocating it, and there were many financial issues they needed to resolve as a result. After 1973, the Grand Prix Committee was no longer listed in the show program, and Baker was eventually removed from the Chagrin Valley PHA Board listing. He continued to design the grand prix course for several years while juggling his job as trainer and traveling to work at other horse shows.

In the Grand Prix Winner's Circle

Bernie Traurig scored his first of two 1970s wins in 1973 at the $7,500 Cleveland Grand Prix aboard a relatively inexperienced mare, Springdale, owned by fashion model Michael Cody. Traurig, twenty-eight, of Morrisville, Pennsylvania, bested Joe Fargis, who piloted Patrick Butler's Old English to second place. A lack of parking turned away some of the estimated sixteen thousand spectators.[50]

Everything about the horse show was to capacity in 1973 as entries soared to 1,100 equines for 107 horse show classes. Management handled the increase well, and a fourth ring was constructed to accommodate the overflow, as well as additional stable tents totaling 135,000 square feet.

By the mid-1970s, the weak economy began impacting the horse world with rising costs for hay, grain, services for veterinarians and farriers and more. Horses were being sold due to upkeep costs, and the show schedules were being trimmed. The Chagrin Valley PHA show, like others, saw a decline; however, since they had already reached maximum horse capacity, it helped ease the numbers.[51]

In 1974, Friendship Farm's Coming Attraction, ridden by top amateur rider Thom Hardy, was victorious as a crowd of seventeen thousand watched. Fences topped six feet in height in the jump-off for the $7,500 Cleveland Grand Prix. The favorite, Sympatico, had broken the indoor high

1973 Cleveland Grand Prix winners Springdale and Bernie Traurig and Leah Stroud (right). *Chagrin Valley PHA Horse Shows Inc.*

jump record the year before at Madison Square Garden, clearing seven feet, four inches, but they couldn't beat Hardy that day.

In 1975, Derby Hill Farm's flashy little chestnut with four white socks and a blaze, Sandsablaze, ridden by nineteen-year-old Buddy Brown from South Salem, New York, upset the big boys in the $10,000 Cleveland Grand Prix. Brown was the newest and youngest member of the USET, and Sandsablaze was a Thoroughbred that didn't make the grade as a racehorse. Of the thirty-seven entries, a whopping nineteen scored faultless first rounds over the big course.

Brown and Sandsablaze bested the favorite, Caesar, ridden by Joe Fargis. Both horses were meticulous, jumping fault-free in three rounds of competition, but Sandsablaze had a faster jump-off time to win. The signature Cleveland Wall was raised to six feet, two inches in the final round. Brown, idolized by teenage girls, drew screams from the crowd as loud as those for show jumping superstar Rodney Jenkins.

1975 Cleveland Grand Prix winners Sandsablaze and Buddy Brown. *Chagrin Valley PHA Horse Shows Inc.*

Among the guests that day was sports magnate Nick Mileti, new owner of the Cleveland Coliseum, who pledged to bring show jumping to his venue. "If an exciting event like today's Prix can draw the kind of crowds I've seen here, rest assured we will have an event like it at the Coliseum as soon as possible," Mileti told the *Plain Dealer*.[52] It was estimated that the seven-day show drew sixty thousand spectators.

Six of the top eight placings were won by one-time USET team members, positioning the United States well for upcoming Olympic games. The annual dates for the Chagrin Valley PHA Horse Show, the fourth week of July, were established on the American Horse Shows Association calendar and not open to alteration. In 1976, the horse show was in the unenviable position of being in direct conflict with the Olympic games in Montreal. Many of the show stables that regularly competed at Cleveland were affected either as participants or spectators. The PHA Committee made the decision not to reduce the level of prize

The Cleveland Zoological Society, one of the beneficiaries, participates in the Cleveland Grand Prix parade. *Chagrin Valley PHA Horse Shows Inc.*

money in spite of the prospect of fewer entries. The games cost the show 163 horses, and there were only 731 entries.

Although the 1976 Cleveland Grand Prix field was reduced to only seventeen competitors, the shows standards remained high, and riders and ten thousand fans were not cheated out of a great competition. The winner of the first 1970 American Gold Cup at the polo field, Conrad Homfeld, twenty-four, of Crozier, Virginia, returned to capture the $10,000 Cleveland Grand Prix aboard the Grand Prix Horse of the Year, Balbuco, owned by Mr. and Mrs. Patrick Butler. He bested a field that included seven clean after two rounds. Barney Ward aboard T.R. was the first to jump clean in 49.1 seconds and remained the leader until Homfeld guided Balbuco to a clean round in 47.1 seconds, leaving Ward to finish in second place.

Course designer Jerry Baker was coaching the Mexican Team at the Olympics, and so Steve Stephens designed courses for the jumpers that week and oversaw the construction of the grand prix course. He made a few alterations to Baker's plans, including removing the water jump from the planned jump-off. He felt the horses were not jumping it well, getting

1976 Cleveland Grand Prix winners Balbuco and Conrad Homfeld. *Chagrin Valley PHA Horse Shows Inc.*

sloppy and landing in it, and the result was they were losing respect for the water. He explained that that could happen if jumped too often, as it is not a difficult obstacle.

Local rider and trainer Gabor Francia-Kiss aboard Kenny King's Royal Blue. *Chagrin Valley PHA Horse Shows Inc.*

The fastest round finished third—trainer Bernie Traurig and The Cardinal clocked an amazing 43.7 seconds in the jump-off but had the top blocks down on the six-foot-one-inch Cleveland Wall. They had been erroneously penalized four faults at the water jump landing in the first round, but that was reversed by the judges. The professional trainer-rider had moved to Northeast Ohio in 1975 to join E.R. Ismond's Hunting Valley Farm in Troy Township, Geauga County. He returned to the Cleveland Grand Prix winner's circle for the second time in 1978, riding the Ismonds' local favorite, The Cardinal. As a horseman, Traurig was known for developing such horses as Idle Dice, Sloopy and the hunter Castle Walk. The Ismonds' daughter, Teddi, was a very successful local rider since her early days in the pony division.

In 1977, fans saw the all-time money-winning grand prix horse, Idle Dice, add the Cleveland Grand Prix to his long list of wins. Redheaded Virginian Rodney Jenkins, who rode in the first Cleveland Grand Prix

1978 Cleveland Grand Prix winners The Cardinal and Bernie Traurig. *Chagrin Valley PHA Horse Shows Inc.*

and won in 1967, returned to the winner's circle a full decade later on another winning Harry Gill entry. While it was a good show for Jenkins, it was not so good for Robert Ridland, who broke his shoulder in a crash and was taken to the Cleveland Clinic. His horses went in the grand prix with substitute riders—Buddy Brown rode Flying John, and Bernie Traurig rode Southside.[53]

Two years later, in 1979, Jenkins returned to claim his third victory riding Edie Spruance's Second Balcony. He closed out the decade and a string of thirteen all-male victories in the Cleveland Grand Prix after the ladies had won in 1965 and 1966. Although show jumping is one of only a few Olympic sports where men and women compete as equals, it was dominated by men during this period.

Cleveland Grand Prix Riders on the Air

In 1977, a number of grand prix riders were interviewed by WBKC Radio 1560 AM of Chardon, Ohio, as a preview of the Cleveland Grand Prix. The interviews, used for talk shows and to promote the upcoming horse show and grand prix, give a glimpse of show jumping in the 1970s. Following are several excerpts.

Interviewer to Rodney Jenkins: What kind of challenge is the Chagrin Valley horse show, and is the Cleveland Grand Prix course difficult?

Jenkins: Chagrin Valley is one of the first horse shows to ever really get grand prix jumping on its feet. I'd call it the founder horse show of the grand prix circuit. It's always a show. It comes at a time of the year when nothing else is going on, so you have most of the good horses from Canada and the United States competing here. It's always one of the best settings, I think. It's a good horse show. I really have nothing bad to say about it. It's very well run. It's very convenient to have places to stay, and there's always good competition, good horses. I'm bringing Alice, Mr. Demeanor and Icy Paws. I don't think the Number One Spy horse will be ready to come there yet, but she would be very good there. A girl called Terry Rudd that rides with me—she might show Mr. Demeanor in the Grand Prix. She rides a lot of my green horses, and she helps me out working. She's very good. When it first started, the Cleveland Grand Prix course was one of the toughest. Now, comparatively speaking, it's just another course on the grand prix circuit—except you have the grab, which is unique; the bank, which is kind of unique; and the jumping set. But all the stuff like that, that's mental problems, not horses. Horses don't pay attention to that kind of thing.

———

Michele McEvoy: This is Michele McEvoy, and I'm from High Hopes Farm, Pinehurst, North Carolina. I have two horses in the grand prix series this year: Night Murmur and Semi-Pro. I think that to become a grand prix rider, it takes years and years of experience and a lot of determination. It's not something you can just hop into because you have a horse that's capable of doing it or because you want to do it. It's a long, basic process where you start off riding in your Preliminary jumpers, which is your first series of jumpers—horses who have won less than $1,000. Then you move into Intermediate—horses that've won less than $3,000—and, finally, your Open. I think that most of the riders showing today in the grand prix jumpers have started as juniors...The Open Jumper division used to be for horses that were erratic and didn't have too many manners. They didn't have to be very rideable; they just had to jump. And the sport is getting so technical and so fine...the jumps are so big and the courses so difficult that it's becoming harder and harder to find grand prix jumpers. Even if you have a top horse, every course you go to is very different. The sport is becoming very popular for spectators, and I hope that it's really going places in the world of spectator sports.

———

Interviewer to Robert Ridland: What do you look for in a horse, and where do you get your horses?

Ridland: You want a very good athlete to begin with...before they can even jump. You want them to be very well balanced, you want a good sense of equilibrium and you want them to be bold. And you work from there. It takes a lot of training, but you have to start with a lot of raw talent. We basically get our horses from the racetrack. 90 percent of our horses in this country are American Thoroughbreds. In Europe, they use a different kind of breed, but we use the Thoroughbred, and we go get them originally from the tracks...I'll be in Cleveland in the grand prix on Southside, a horse that was in the Montreal Olympics.

———

Katie Monahan: I'm from Bloomfield Hills, Michigan, and I'm riding a horse called The Jones Boy. We started out the year in Florida. We do the Florida circuit, which consists of four shows and then a big jumping grand prix at Tampa Stadium. I used The Jones Boy in that particular class, and he went well but had four faults. We've been traveling up and down the East Coast now since March, and we go in July to the Chagrin Valley Horse Show, which is one of the biggest shows of the year because it is in the Midwest and draws people from the East and the West, so it's considered one of the biggest shows. We all look forward to Chagrin because of the big grand prix that is held there every year. It's a great competition; the best jumpers in the country are there, and it's usually a very exciting class. And this year, with The Jones Boy, I'm looking forward to that particularly because he's very good in a big field like the Chagrin course, and I think he has a chance to do quite well if I ride well.

Gene Mische Returns to Cleveland Horse Shows

The 1975 and 1976 Chagrin Valley PHA Horse Show program's list of judges included former Cleveland trainer Eugene R. Mische of Palmetto, Florida. In 1977, Mische was listed as course designer of jumpers, the Hunter Derby and the Cleveland Grand Prix. It was the first year Jerry Baker's name was absent from the program. In 1978, the Chagrin Valley PHA Horse Show was "Presented by Stadium Jumping," and Mische was listed in the new role of manager. The course designer for the $10,000 Cleveland Grand Prix was internationally renowned Pamela Carruthers from Chippenham, England.

Eugene "Gene" Mische grew up in Cleveland and worked under horseman Scotty Donaldson at the Cleveland Cavalry's Troop A Riding Academy. After attending law school and working as an accountant, he became a trainer and farm manager for Charlie Rohr in Ohio. In the late 1950s, his résumé states that he left Cleveland for West Palm Beach with

1978 course designer Pamela Carruthers and official Herbert Lytle. *Chagrin Valley PHA Horse Shows Inc.*

Gene Mische (center) at the Chagrin Valley Hunter Trials. *Chuck Kinney collection.*

twenty-six dollars and two horses. He started his career training for such noted owners as Patrick Butler and worked with such riders as Rodney Jenkins and Steve Stephens.[54]

Mische began organizing horse shows in Florida and was president of the Central Florida Hunter/Jumper Association in 1964 and 1965. He started the Sunshine Circuit, a series of horse shows that encouraged competitors to show in Florida during the winter. He went on to found Stadium Jumping Inc., which grew to become the nation's top producer of hunter/jumper horse shows.

Throughout his career, he never forgot his roots, and his family remained based in Cleveland. Mische continued developing horse shows in his hometown and worked with Nick Mileti to create an indoor horse show at the Coliseum in Richfield, Ohio, the Cleveland National. Mische envisioned that the October show would make Cleveland the first stop on the Indoor Fall Circuit, and it included a grand prix—the $10,000 U.S. National Open Jumping Championship. The executive committee included many of the committee members from the Chagrin Valley PHA show, including

Stanley Stone, Charles Kinney, Howard Lewis and Karen Schneider. The Coliseum horse show returned the following year as the Ohio National, but the expensive endeavor made it impossible to continue, and the U.S. Open Jumping Championship relocated to another venue.

When Mische was seeking sponsor support for the American Invitational in Florida, he approached show jumping supporter August Busch Jr. about the potential involvement of his company, Anheuser-Busch. Busch mentioned that the invitational was a great idea but said that Anheuser-Busch would be better represented on a national level. That feedback led Mische to further development of the national grand prix tour concept.

Stadium Jumping's management expanded outside Florida, and Mische saw the opportunity to link the grand prix in a series. In the mid-1970s, the U.S. Grand Prix Series recognized year-end leaders of horses, riders and owners, and participating events were originally located in Florida, Virginia, Connecticut, New York, Pennsylvania and Washington, D.C., along with Chagrin Valley's Cleveland Grand Prix.

The Grand Prix Series concept was formalized in 1978 when sixteen of the nation's top grand prix became part of the American Grand Prix Association (AGA), which was founded by Mische, Frank Chapot, Leonard King, Larry Langer and Joshua Barney. The nonprofit organization promoted the highest caliber of show jumping in the United States, and the tour launched with a total of $247,000 in prize money split among the sixteen events.

In 1978, the $10,000 Cleveland Grand Prix was stop number eleven in the inaugural series that started in February in Jacksonville. The $25,000 American Invitational in Tampa was the last of four Florida shows before competitors traveled to Pennsylvania for the Valley Forge and Devon events. Afterward, they went on to Upperville, Virginia; Ox Ridge in Darien, Connecticut; the now-defunct North American Grand Prix in Bloomfield Hills, Michigan; and Lake Placid's I Love New York Grand Prix before heading to Cleveland.

The tour picked up in late August for two events in Syosset, New York, before returning to Pennsylvania for the $32,000 American Gold Cup. It then traveled to the $35,000 American Jumping Derby in Newport, Rhode Island, and culminated in October with the U.S. Open Jumping Championships in Charlotte, North Carolina.

Adding to the prestige of the AGA series were the year-end awards for Rider of the Year and Horse of the Year. In 1978, an AGA Lady Rider of the Year was also awarded, as was the custom of the day. It was presented

Hatless Melanie Smith and Radnor II. *Chagrin Valley PHA Horse Shows Inc.*

only in 1978, and Melanie Smith won both the AGA Rider of the Year and Lady Rider of the Year titles that year. Her horse, Val de Loire, owned by Still Meadow Farm, was named Horse of the Year.

Karen Schneider, who headed the Box Seat Committee of the Chagrin Valley PHA Horse Show and became chairwoman in the 1990s, shared with the author: "I hosted a meeting with Gene Mische, Leah Stroud and Stanley Stone, and Bud Stanner of IMG (International Management Group) was there. They wanted the first grand prix to be part of the new AGA series, and because we helped make that happen…Gene never charged Cleveland the franchise fee that came with being a part of the AGA series."

Cleveland connections helped Mische promote the sport and gain valuable television and marketing opportunities. In addition to retaining James Passant's Cleveland public relations agency, Carlton & Douglas, the AGA and the Cleveland-based International Management Group (IMG) announced an agreement for exclusive promotion, marketing and television rights for AGA member events, including the Cleveland Grand

Prix.[55] IMG's H. Kent "Bud" Stanner said in a news release: "IMG is very pleased with its new relationship with the American Grand Prix Association, as we feel that show jumping is truly one of the emerging sports that encompasses enthusiasm of most Americans for competitions which have natural surroundings and spontaneous excitement."

The AGA series impacted the Cleveland Grand Prix greatly because the television coverage expanded the notoriety of the Chagrin Valley even farther. In 1979, the Cleveland Grand Prix prize money jumped from $10,000 to $25,000, with the winner's share jumping from $2,500 to $7,000. The Chagrin Valley PHA Horse Show, still managed by Mische and presented by Stadium Jumping, drew new interest from potential corporate sponsors.

Chapter 8

THE 1980s:
WELCOMING SPONSORS, MANAGING
COMPETITION AND CHANGE

G ene's plan was that by organizing the grand prix into a larger entity, the sport could attract more sponsors and give the sponsors more exposure and benefits," said Michael Morrissey of Stadium Jumping Inc. After initial sponsorship by Carte Blanche, Mercedes-Benz of North America became the American Grand Prix Association title sponsor for the 1981 tour, which began a period of accelerated growth. In 1985, the Mercedes-Benz Grand Prix Series of Show Jumping offered over $1.5 million in prize money and year-end awards with thirty-two events spanning the United States in twenty-five major metropolitan areas. More spectators were exposed to the sport due to increased publicity and television coverage provided by ESPN, which covered ten events in 1985, broadcasting to more than 34 million households. Show jumping grew in terms of horses and riders, and reduced entry fees kept costs under control for the owners. In 1978, there were 46 riders competing on the inaugural AGA tour. By 1985, that number had grown to 194, due in part to series expansion to include West Coast events in 1981.[56]

In 1980, the Chagrin Valley Horse Show and $25,000 Cleveland Grand Prix welcomed its first title sponsor, Prescott, Ball & Turben. The investment firm promoted its name on the horse show, as well as in the name of the Cleveland Grand Prix. Because Cleveland was a very popular stop with riders and owners, Stadium Jumping added a second week to the schedule with a new hunter/jumper show, the Cleveland Metro Classic, and managed both shows. The Metro Classic ran the week prior to the Chagrin Valley

PHA Horse Show and culminated with a $5,000 Chagrin Valley Jumper Classic, a perfect primer and complement to the Cleveland Grand Prix.

In addition to the local support from Prescott, Ball & Turben, the Cleveland Grand Prix also carried the name of sponsors affiliated with the American Grand Prix Association. A special VIP ringside chalet was erected to host sponsors entertaining clients and guests with catered food, an open bar and take-home gifts. The Cleveland Grand Prix ticket became even more prestigious in the VIP chalet, and the course designers often planned obstacles to give guests a special view of the action.

The guests also had the best seats to view the traditional pre–grand prix festivities that were introduced at the first Cleveland Grand Prix in 1965 and carried on by Stadium Jumping. Festivities varied each year but usually featured exhibitions of top local horsemanship spotlighting dressage, local carriage clubs carrying show officials or honored guests of the show, the Chagrin Valley Hunt members and hounds and, on occasion, members of the polo team. Depending on the weather, a parade of riders circled the field and on at least one occasion provided added thrills when bagpipers set off a few bucking, spooking horses. Musical performances from local groups or high school bands entertained while spectators found their seats or, if they were tailgating from the back of a vehicle, opened up picnic baskets. Mische raised the level of entertainment with special guests such as trumpeter Doc Severinsen from television's *Tonight Show* fame. A color guard from the Cleveland Mounted Police or Cleveland Metroparks Rangers preceded the playing of the national anthem, and the traditional ringmaster called the first horse to course.

With the new sponsor involvement, Sunday's grand prix became more colorful as banners were added around the show ring promoting the businesses. The jumps also had a new look, as many carried sponsor logos and emblems. During the 1980s, as sponsorship grew, so did the sponsor presence, and course designers added custom jumps such as the Anheuser-Busch jumps that were flanked by giant Budweiser beer bottles and Shamu whales representing Sea World, which was owned by Anheuser-Busch.

In 1980, Leah Stroud took over leadership of the Chagrin Valley PHA Horse Show Board as chairwoman, and Stanley Stone became co-chairman as the growing horse show became harder to manage for the volunteer committees. Schneider said:

> *I always liked Gene, and his heart was with Cleveland. As he got involved with our show, Leah and Stan lost their say in running it and their authority*

and split off from the Stadium Jumping operation. In 1983, they moved the Chagrin Valley PHA Horse Show to the George M. Humphrey Equestrian Center of Lake Erie College in Concord Township to create a smaller, more manageable show with no grand prix. Gene continued to run his show and the Cleveland Grand Prix at the Polo Field. Hugh Kincannon, who had Ridgewood Stables in Medina, managed the Chagrin Valley PHA Horse Show at Lake Erie. After a few years there, Hugh and Leah were searching for a ring and facility better suited to the show, so it was moved to Ridgewood Stables for a short time. That was too far away, though, and lost the connection to the Chagrin Valley. In 1990, Chagrin Valley Farms in Bainbridge Township was growing and improving—Leah liked the facility and the idea of getting it back closer to home and its origin, so they leased the facility for the Chagrin Valley PHA to run the show there.

Cleveland Grand Prix Action

In 1980, New York's Debbie Shaffner scored her first major win at the $25,000 Cleveland Grand Prix aboard the grey stallion Abdullah. Shaffner was the first woman to win the event since 1966. In later years, Debbie Shaffner Stephens reflected:

My winning the Cleveland Grand Prix aboard Abdullah is a very memorable career point because it was the first grand prix either of us ever entered. I had been a hunter rider and started working with Abdullah because he wasn't succeeding as an event horse. I worked him up and felt he was ready for a grand prix when he went to Cleveland. I remember that day well because it was a big field and there were so many famous riders like Rodney Jenkins and Bernie Traurig. I was awed. I knew I would have to risk it all to win, and Abdullah's owners [Williamsburg Farm and Sue Williams] *were behind me, so I could go for it. It was the rainiest day ever, and my reins kept slipping—plus we were on the grass—but he felt great. It was a fairy tale to go into my first grand prix on a day like that and win.*[57]

While he was busy building the show jumping series around the country, Mische continued to manage the Cleveland horse show, focusing on a single week in 1981. With ongoing support from Prescott, Ball & Turben, the

1980 Cleveland Grand Prix winners Abdullah and Debbie Shaffner. *Sue Williams collection.*

Cleveland Grand Prix was elevated to a $30,000 purse, with $9,000 going to the winner.

The 1981 winner was the popular former Clevelander Michael Matz aboard F. Eugene Dixon's Jet Run. When Matz won the Cleveland Grand Prix in 1972 aboard Rosie Report, he had been riding for J. Basil Ward's Hounds Hill Stables for just a year. Matz went on to international success representing the United States in the Montreal Olympic games in 1976 aboard Grande. The team finished fourth that year. Unfortunately, the boycott of the 1980 Olympic games in Moscow kept the team from attending; however, when he returned to win the Cleveland Grand Prix in 1981, Matz was the reigning World Cup champion, having won in Birmingham, England, earlier in the year with Jet Run.

The Cleveland Grand Prix was soggy that year, with standing water on the field due to heavy rain. Efforts to dry the field by burning gasoline were unsuccessful. Eleven riders withdrew because of the conditions, reducing the field to twenty-two entries. The experienced Thoroughbred Jet Run had found his way to show jumping after a failed career on the racetrack. The

1981 Cleveland Grand Prix winners Jet Run and Michael Matz. *Chagrin Valley PHA Horse Shows Inc.*

bad footing didn't keep him from a clean first round, along with eleven other horses. In the jump-off, they were nearly a second faster than second-place Eadenvale and Bernie Traurig.[58]

The win in Cleveland helped the pair earn AGA honors in 1981 as Rider of the Year, and Jet Run was named AGA Horse of the Year. Leonard King, president of the AGA, recalled presenting the award to Jet Run's owner, F. Eugene Dixon, the former owner of both the Philadelphia Flyers hockey team and 76ers professional basketball team. "The awards were at Madison Square Garden, and the AGA sponsor, Mercedes-Benz, gave the riders financial gifts based on their points. We were dressed in our evening scarlet and went into the ring, where Fitz Dixon was awarded a new Mercedes-Benz. As we were leaving the ring, he said to me, 'We have to do something about the ring in Devon,'" chuckled King to the author. Today, the show ring at the Devon, Pennsylvania grounds is still called the Dixon Oval.

The impact of the AGA series on the sport was huge. Owners and riders planned their schedules around key events as they sought points for year-end honors in addition to the individual grand prix awards. The tour attracted sponsors who wanted to be affiliated with the sport and use the events for lavish entertainment of clients and potential clients—it gave them a chance to provide a VIP experience in their own backyard.

Katie Monahan aboard Tom Simmons. *Chagrin Valley PHA Horse Shows Inc.*

In 1982, Katie Monahan was having an exceptional year on the tour. In the $30,000 Cleveland Grand Prix, she entered two very different horses: the French Normandy stallion, Noren, and Joe Wyant's big chestnut gelding, Jethro. Jethro had four faults in the first round, but Noren was the only horse of the class to score double clean rounds and a victory over Anthony D'Ambrosio Jr. and Sugar Ray. Other horses in the field that year included future Olympic mounts Touch of Class and Abdullah. Monahan and Noren went on to earn year-end AGA honors for both Rider and Horse of the Year.

Monahan returned to Cleveland in 1983 with both Noren and Jethro, but it was Jethro's turn to win the Cleveland Grand Prix at the Prescott Hunter/ Jumper Classic. The petite Monahan showed her skill riding the large horse, often referred to as the gentle giant.

She returned in 1984 as a favorite defending her back-to-back Cleveland Grand Prix wins. She was one of only five women in the male-dominated field. Monahan and Michael Matz, the second Cleveland favorite, had both been passed over for selection to the U.S. Olympic show jumping team in Los Angeles. In 1984, the winner of the $35,000 Prescott Cleveland Grand Prix was not the favorite, however. It was an Olympic veteran from the 1960 Rome Silver Medal U.S. Equestrian Team, George Morris.

1984 Cleveland Grand Prix winners Brussels and George Morris. *Stadium Jumping Inc.*

During the Cleveland Grand Prix, it appeared the win belonged to Norman Dello Joio and the French stallion I Love You, the duo that had captured the 1983 FEI World Cup the prior year. Dello Joio, who was an alternate on the 1984 U.S. Olympic Team, was the fastest in the jump-off following a first round with thirty-seven starters. The final challengers on course, George Morris and the grey mare Brussels, beat the time for the win. He also finished third aboard his earlier ride, Rio. Morris, forty-six, had returned to the show jumping circuit the prior year after an absence of nearly twenty years. The man who coached many of the successful show jumping riders and four of the five riders named to the 1984 Olympic team let the fans know he wasn't ready to put away his show clothes.

In 1984, the United States hosted the Olympic games in Los Angeles, California. In front of record live and television audiences, the U.S. Equestrian Team shined bright. The show jumping team earned its first equestrian team gold medal with stellar performances by Joe Fargis aboard Touch of Class, Leslie Burr aboard Albany, Conrad Homfeld on Abdullah

1984 gold medal U.S. Olympic Show Jumping Team. *From left to right*: Joe Fargis, Leslie Burr, Conrad Homfeld and Melanie Smith. *TishQuirk/Show Jumping Hall of Fame.*

and Melanie Smith on Calypso. They were coached by a former Cleveland Grand Prix winner, Chef d'Equipe Frank Chapot. In individual Olympic show jumping, the United States was also victorious when Joe Fargis and Touch of Class earned the gold medal and Conrad Homfeld and Abdullah earned the silver. Cleveland fans had a special connection to the Olympic games since they had seen the horses, riders and their coach compete in their Chagrin Valley backyard during the Cleveland Grand Prix.

Following a stellar showcase of Olympic show jumping talent, the 1985 $35,000 Prescott Cleveland Grand Prix hosted a field of fifty-five entries. The growth of the AGA and its incentives, plus encouragement of young and up-and-coming riders, created a surge of entries. The jump order featured such top names as Olympic gold medalists Melanie Smith and Calypso, as well as seasoned riders on young horses and rookie riders making their grand prix debut. There were even a few local riders in the large field that included horses from the West Coast. Cleveland audiences

1986 Cleveland Grand Prix winners Albany and Debbie Dolan. *Chagrin Valley PHA Horse Shows Inc.*

who were accustomed to familiar names were introduced to many new names that year.

In 1985, Norman Dello Joio of South Salem, New York, returned looking to improve on his second-place finish the prior year. "Stormin' Norman," the son of a famous composer, and the Dutch chestnut gelding Corsair poured on early speed. Linda Allen's grand prix course reduced the starting field to ten, and Dello Joio and Corsair jumped off second in the order. Their clean time held until the end, with the only faster round, Kara Hanley aboard Fight Back, pulling a rail. The win earned them $10,000.

In 1986, Canadian course designer Robert Jolicoeur brought his creativity to the Cleveland Grand Prix. Young Debbie Dolan of Oyster Bay, New York, had a local fan club of Cleveland relatives and owned two of the horses in the grand prix. Her ten-year-old Thoroughbred, Albany, jumped the course with room to spare over the jumps and bested the five-horse jump-off to win. Albany had been part of the 1984 Olympic gold medal team, ridden then by Dolan's trainer, Leslie Burr-Lenehan.

In 1987, the hottest pair in the AGA series was rookie Greg Best, twenty-three, of Flemington, New Jersey, and the nine-year-old grey gelding Gem Twist, owned by Michael Golden. Best was a student of Frank Chapot, and Gem Twist was sired by Chapot's horse, Good Twist. During the $50,000 Prescott Cleveland Grand Prix, the field of forty-six entries was trimmed to seven clean rounds over Steve Stephens's demanding course, and seventeen horses scored four faults in the first round to tie for eighth place. After a fall in the first round aboard another horse, Louis Jacobs and Desiree scored the first clean round of the tiebreaker and held until Best returned to trim off two seconds for the win. The $15,000 winner's purse contributed to Best winning the American Grand Prix Association Rookie of the Year, and Gem Twist was named AGA Horse of the Year. The USET Selection Committee was in attendance at Cleveland to decide the United States team for the Pan American Games in Indianapolis the following month. The Cleveland win clinched Best's being named to the team.

The following year, the number of horses in the 1988 $50,000 Cleveland Grand Prix was reduced to twenty-six due to the Olympic selection trials. The Cleveland Grand Prix, an observation trial where the selection committee was in attendance, preceded the final mandated trial to decide the team. Many of the sixteen short-listed riders elected to save their horses to prepare for that event. Greg Best and Gem Twist were among the absentees from the 1988 Cleveland Grand Prix. Instead, they attended the mandated Seoul

1987 Cleveland Grand Prix winners Gem Twist and Greg Best. *Chagrin Valley PHA Horse Shows Inc.*

Olympic Trials, which eventually resulted in Best earning two silver medals (individual and team) at the Olympic games.

However, eleven thousand Cleveland fans were treated to an Olympic-caliber course set by England's Richard Jeffery and a preview of a world

Madison Square Garden American Grand Prix Association Horse of the Year presentation, 1987. *From left to right*: Art Pepin, Elizabeth Busch Burke, Michael Golden, Gene Mische, Greg Best (with Gem Twist) and Frank Chapot. *Stadium Jumping Inc.*

champion in the making when a talented twenty-four-year-old from Wisconsin scored her biggest career win to date. Elizabeth "Beezie" Patton (later Madden), a student of Katie Monahan, rode Northern Magic to top the Cleveland Grand Prix's six-horse jump-off, gaining valuable experience for future international fame that would come later in the World Cup, World Championships and Olympic games.

Wisconsin provided the winner of the 1989 $50,000 Prescott Cleveland Grand Prix as well. This time it was Donald Cheska from Waukesha, riding the Irish-bred Dury Lad. The day's heat and humidity took their toll on the thirty-eight starters, with only six clean after round two. A daring ride cutting many corners resulted in Cheska finishing six seconds ahead of his closest challenger, Michael Dorman and The Empress, and with a well-deserved victory.

During the 1980s, the United States earned a reputation as a world power in show jumping. In addition to the double gold medals and one silver at the 1984 Olympic games, the USET brought home double silver medals at the 1988 Olympic games and dominated the international FEI World Cup Show Jumping Championship with seven straight U.S. victories from 1980 to 1987.

Chapter 9

THE 1990S:
CONFLICTS, CANCELLATION
AND A COMEBACK

The 1980s signaled an end to Prescott, Ball & Turben's sponsorship agreement for the Cleveland Grand Prix and the horse show. Prescott enjoyed success and was pleased during its involvement. Changes in management and marketing focus impacted sponsorship direction within the AGA series as well, and new sponsors joined the tour. Although Stadium Jumping did not have a title sponsor for its five-day horse show at the Polo Field, the $35,000 Johnnie Walker Cleveland Grand Prix had the support of a new AGA sponsor, and giant scotch bottles flanked a jump on the grand prix course in 1990. British rider James Young and Boysie II emerged the victors from the thirty-seven-horse field. Illinois rider Chris Kappler, twenty-three, rode Concorde to finish second.

The following Saturday, Kappler was in Cincinnati, Ohio, to win the $100,000 Grand Prix of Cincinnati with Concorde before driving back to the Chagrin Valley to win the new the $15,000 Chagrin Valley Jumper Classic aboard Warrant. The event was part of the Chagrin Valley PHA Horse Show, newly relocated to the175-acre Chagrin Valley Farms Horse Show Complex.

In 1991, Stadium Jumping and the Chagrin Valley PHA packaged their two weeks under the National Equestrian Festival banner. The partnership was beneficial in boosting entries for both shows as they attracted riders with two AGA events: the $25,000 Cleveland Grand Prix at Chagrin Valley Farms on July 14 and the $35,000 Michelob U.S. Open Jumping Championship presented by Johnnie Walker on July 21 at the Cleveland Metroparks Polo

1990 Cleveland Grand Prix winners Oxo and Peter Leone. *Stadium Jumping Inc.*

Field. The following week, riders could easily travel south to Cincinnati for the AGA tour's next stop at the $75,000 American Jumping Classic.

It was the only time in its history that organizers ran the Cleveland Grand Prix at a location other than the Polo Field. The new location hosted thirty-eight horses, and the grand prix was won by Peter Leone aboard his chestnut, Oxo. The victory was remarkable because the pair had been sidelined for almost two years. Leone, thirty, of Franklin Lakes, New Jersey, withdrew from the AGA tour in 1989 to concentrate on his professional career. His brothers Mark and Armand continued to ride Oxo until a severe tendon injury in April 1990 threatened to end his show ring career.[59]

The following week, Leone and Oxo triumphed again, making it two weeks in a row at the $35,000 U.S. Open Jumper Championship, which had relocated to Cleveland from Palm Beach, Florida. A field of forty-eight horses competed in front of ESPN television cameras. The AGA series was once again sponsored by Budweiser, which influenced ESPN show jumping coverage, as Elizabeth Busch Burke continued her late father, August Busch Jr.'s, support of show jumping.

In 1992, Miami, Florida's Margie Goldstein began what would be a twenty-year reign as the queen of the Cleveland Grand Prix. The two-time AGA Rider of the Year bested a field of thirty-four starters aboard Daydream to win the 1992 $30,000 Cleveland Grand Prix. The course at the historic Cleveland Metroparks Polo Field was wet, and slippery turf played a factor in the twelve-horse jump-off, causing a fall from sixteen-year-old Rookie of the Year McLain Ward. Goldstein set the time to beat when she returned sixth in the order, and Peter Leone and Oxo finished second. Goldstein later recalled, "He was the first horse I ever had that was competitive in the grand prix ring, and he has a special place in my heart. I won my first grand prix on him in 1986 in Cincinnati, and he's averaged about $60,000 in earnings every year since."[60]

Many of the grand prix riders stayed the week for the $50,000 U.S. Open Jumping Championship, which had twenty-eight starters. Leone and his sixteen-year-old Belgian-bred Oxo took home the blue ribbon for the second year in a row. George Lindemann Jr. finished second aboard Cellular Farms' Abound, and McLain Ward was third aboard his father's horse, Just Guess, after the eleven-horse jump-off.

In 1993, AGA Rider of the Year Susie Hutchison, a veteran California pro, scored double wins at the $30,000 Cleveland Grand Prix and the $50,000

1993 Cleveland Grand Prix winners Samsung Woodstock and Susie Hutchison. *Chagrin Valley PHA Horse Shows Inc.*

U.S. Open Jumping Championship, both aboard Samsung Woodstock at the Polo Field. The talented horse's unconventional bitless bridle made fans look twice. Hutchison's trainer of thirty-five years, the legendary Jimmy Williams, was sidelined with a trip to the Cleveland Clinic hospital for angioplasty surgery. He was released in time to see her win the final event at the Polo Field, the U.S. Open.[61]

Conflict and Cancellation

In 1994, the invitations were already printed for a special thirtieth anniversary party to celebrate the Cleveland Grand Prix when Stadium Jumping announced it would cancel its horse show. The $30,000 class was scheduled for July 17, but on May 12, 1994 the *Chagrin Valley Times'* front-page headline read, "Horse Shows Skip Valley—America's Oldest Grand Prix Cancelled." Gene Mische told the newspaper the major issue was a date conflict. "We have a strong following in this area, and I'm sure there will be a large number of fans, as well as competitors. Sorry to hear about the cancellation," he said.[62]

The U.S. Open Jumping Championship grand prix was relocated to another show, and the Chagrin Valley PHA Horse Show continued at Chagrin Valley Farms, but the Cleveland Grand Prix was cancelled. "Traditionally, it's been an unlucky week weather-wise, and it always seems to rain, which causes poor footing because the show is held on grass. It's sad, but it certainly must have affected the finances," former Ohio PHA president Beth Nielsen told the newspaper.

The "Commentary" column for the *Chagrin Valley Times* that week was titled "Claim to Fame Takes a Break." The commentary called the Cleveland Grand Prix the Chagrin Valley's greatest claim to fame, adding:

> *While that may not be earth-shattering news to the general public, the Cleveland Grand Prix focuses a lot of attention from the international equestrian community on this little corner of the world. It regularly draws some of the world's and nation's top riders to the Chagrin Valley and attracts more media attention here than any other single event. Staging an event of the caliber and prominence of the Cleveland Grand Prix is a major financial undertaking, one that has been especially difficult in recent years because of poor weather. While organizers are confident that the event will*

return to Moreland Hills next year, the long-term future may depend on a major corporate backer.

Karen Schneider noted:

Running the show at the Polo Field was expensive for Gene, and he lost money. There were a lot of expenses running the show at the Cleveland Metroparks Polo Field—even with sponsors it began to cost too much. After he lost the support of his title sponsor, Prescott, Ball & Turben, he didn't have anyone else to step up, but he ran the show anyway. Gene really left after trouble with Mother Nature—that was the real killer. If he could have made money, he would have stayed and continued to run the show in Cleveland. I remember the last year when it rained and it was so wet at the Polo Field they brought helicopters in to try to dry the field for the grand prix—he took a major loss because of the weather, and the date conflict with the World Championship was the final factor to cancel at the Polo Field.

In 1994, Leah Stroud was chairwoman of the Chagrin Valley Horse Show during a rough transition year. The traditional Chagrin Valley PHA Horse Show had leased the Chagrin Valley Farms Horse Show Complex for its venue, and the all-weather rings allowed the show to go on in poor weather. However, when the weather cooperated, there was no location that could match the atmosphere, history and prestige of the Cleveland Metroparks Polo Field.

Although a number of local sponsors of individual classes and divisions supported the show, with sponsorship fees averaging in the $100 to $1,000 range, it wasn't enough to support the higher purses needed to compete with other top horse shows. Without the partnership of the Cleveland Grand Prix, the AGA series or Stadium Jumping's management skill and sponsor connections, it was difficult to attract competitors from outside the area. The Chagrin Valley PHA show was dwindling as a for-profit venture.

Stroud was a strong and respected leader in the horse community, a horsewoman with a strong focus on running a traditional horse show. She admittedly was not skilled in working with sponsors, so they sought outside assistance from a Cleveland marketing sponsorship firm that worked to locate and retain future sponsors for the show. Because of the reputation of the sport and the Cleveland Grand Prix, the firm was confident it would be successful. However, without a passion for horses and a clear understanding of marketing the sport and what it could provide sponsors, the firm was not successful. There were no new sponsors on the horizon to ease the financial burden.

In 1994, the Chagrin Valley was dealt a second blow when the Chagrin Valley PHA announced that the horse show and the Cleveland Grand Prix were cancelled for 1995. "We made the decision because there were a number of things we had to do to rebuild the horse show and concluded it had to move back to the Polo Field after improvements to the rings and facility. As a team, the board decided we had to take a year off; however, we never stopped working," said Schneider.

Staging a Comeback

The board and the Chagrin Valley equestrian community united, bringing together talent and connections to make changes so the show would continue in the future. Leah Stroud was joined by co-chairman Karen Schneider, who had been involved with the show and Stadium Jumping for many years. She had a business approach developed by working in the family's Schneider's Saddlery business, as well as her role as a Gates Mills councilwoman. Board member and attorney Tom Visconsi Jr. assisted with changing the show to a nonprofit entity, as well as reinforcing some of the organization's policies. For example, the Cleveland Grand Prix name had been copyrighted, but in recent years, the name had been interchanged with a July Cleveland car race, sometimes causing confusion among media and spectators. The board contacted race organizers to clear up the name usage, and the car race began using the name Grand Prix of Cleveland.

"We decided to change the structure and mission of the horse show to make it a nonprofit organization. In addition to our board of directors, we created a Provisional Board to expand the number of people involved directly with running the show. Among the additions to the new board were active individuals with business and sponsor connections, marketing skills and local trainers involved in the horse industry," said Schneider. The goals of the Chagrin Valley PHA Horse Show were to run a first-class horse show, raise money for local charity and educate the public. As they planned for the future, those goals were front and center, and a large network of volunteers was recruited to join the team and help run the horse show.

One of the first steps initiated in 1994 was improving the Cleveland Metroparks Polo Field show grounds by installing all-weather surfaces to alleviate problems from the uncontrollable rain and allow the show to go on safely. According to the Cleveland Metroparks manager of Visitor Services, Mike Barnhart, the CVPHA approached the park about bringing its show back to the polo field and enhancing the riding rings by expanding the size and adding an all-weather surface. Barnhart said:

The primary beneficiary, Fieldstone Farm Therapeutic Riding Center of Bainbridge, hosted the competition for riders with disabilities. *Chagrin Valley PHA Horse Shows Inc.*

After gaining approval from groups that hold events at the Metroparks Polo Field, the PHA raised the money for the project and hired an outside contractor for the work. It was a cooperative venture, with the Metroparks supervising the approvals and specifications to assure that it met our requirements. It's a win-win situation because the enhancements benefit the individuals and private groups who use the South Chagrin Reservation's Polo Field—that includes many equestrians and dog owners. This benefits taxpayers without taxpayer dollars.[63]

Construction of two all-weather hunter rings and adjacent warm-up areas was achieved through a $60,000 grant by the William Bingham Foundation, a private philanthropic charity. Bingham Foundation trustee Perry Blossom said, "This capital improvement is seen as a major component to the success of the [KeyBank] Hunter Jumper Classic and its ability to raise funds for local charities."

The weeklong July show's primary beneficiaries were the local nonprofit Therapeutic Riding Center (TRC) and the United States Equestrian Team. The TRC was in the process of conducting its "Little Victories" campaign to raise $3.5 million to build a permanent facility in Bainbridge Township. It was operating at a small stable in Newbury and had plans for a state-of-the-art facility on forty-five acres that would allow the program to expand its services to approximately one thousand students with disabilities per year. The horse show committed to host special classes for riders with disabilities to compete at the Polo Field.

Back in Business

The board made another essential achievement on the way to the comeback when it obtained title sponsorship for the horse show from Society National Bank, which was completing a transition and name change to KeyBank. The new KeyBank Hunter Jumper Classic and its $30,000 KeyBank Cleveland Grand Prix helped reinforce the name with an important Northeast Ohio audience. The horse show's nonprofit status and mission also resonated well with the bank.

"We are extremely delighted to bring championship equestrian competition back to the Northeast Ohio region," said Yank Heisler, president of Society National Bank. "We are proud that through our title sponsorship, local equestrian aficionados and amateur riders will be able to enjoy the sights and competitive spirit that this sporting event offers."[64] Julia Adamsen, senior vice-president and director of marketing for KeyBank, added, "With any sponsorship, we look for events where people feel passionately about a particular sport. And this particular sport has such an enthusiastic following. KeyBank is pleased to be the title sponsor. This sponsorship will create awareness of our private bank and investment services area."[65]

Additional corporate sponsors signed on, including Andersen Consulting, which planned to occupy a ringside chalet for entertainment during competition. "The horse show provides a great opportunity for us to know our clients away from the workplace. Rather than taking executives away from their families to watch a ball game or concert, this type of event allows them to bring their spouses and children to a very relaxed country setting to watch world-class competition," said Earl Slater, partner at Andersen Consulting.[66]

Boosting the Local Economy

According to the American Horse Council's data from 1994, horse shows were generating over $223 million nationally per year. In Ohio, horses are a major industry with the sixth-largest horse population in the United States. With more than 371,000 horses statewide, Ohioans spent more than $703 million in annual maintenance costs for their horses and another $137 million on support services and products in 1994.[67]

The Chagrin Valley was built around a love of horses—you don't have to ride or own horses to be impacted by the equestrian heritage. In 1996, the community embraced the return of the show. Merchants in the nearby village of Chagrin Falls decorated windows with equestrian themes; the local newspaper, the *Chagrin Valley Times*, took over production of the souvenir program at no cost to the board; and fans bought up available box seats.

The absence of the event increased recognition of the impact of the horse show on the local economy—an estimated $2 million infused into the Chagrin Valley. It was estimated the five hundred horses brought with them an average of three people per horse and with them hotel stays, dining, shopping and other economic benefits. Additionally, spectators to horse show also visited the beautiful Chagrin Valley and spent additional dollars.

Since the first Cleveland Grand Prix in 1965, national interest in show jumping had led to an increase of more than one hundred grand prix across the nation. Many of the events were on the American Grand Prix Association tour or a newer tour, the National Grand Prix League. "There are so many more shows now, and we have to work very hard to make the entries want to come. But we have always been known for being nice to our exhibitors. The Valley has always generously supported the show, and we expect it will be the same this year," said Stroud.[68]

Back in Action

In 1996, the CVPHA board hired an experienced manager, Mike Rheinheimer, to focus on running the horse show, and he designed the jumper courses while Howard Lewis designed the hunter courses. Among the 1996 horse show officials were a few connections dating back to the first Cleveland Grand Prix: Mrs. Ernest M. (Betty) Oare, who had competed aboard Navy Commander, was a judge, and Ken Kraus, who had shown in the junior jumpers in 1965, was a jumper judge and announcer.

The $30,000 KeyBank Cleveland Grand Prix was the perfect culmination to the comeback celebration week. Thanks to the sponsor support, it was the largest purse the local organizers had ever offered for the Cleveland Grand Prix. A field of twenty-five entries jumped the first round with several obstacles set at the maximum height of five feet. Only ten horses jumped clean, and among them were AGA Rider of the Year Margie Goldstein and Columbian Equestrian Team show jumper Roberto Gonzalez. However, it was Illinois rider Todd Minikus and Yankee Zulu who grabbed the lead and held it for the win. Yankee Zulu, a seven-year-old German-bred, was actually the least experienced of Minikus's four entries. Margie Goldstein-Engle finished second, and Gonzalez was third.

One of the jumps on course featured a bright red key created to duplicate the sponsor's logo, and that jump would be a fixture on the Cleveland Grand Prix courses for the next three years as KeyBank continued its sponsorship through the rest of the decade. The CVPHA Horse Show met all of KeyBank's sponsor requirements, including a steady increase of attendance figures over each year, so the company extended its sponsorship commitment beyond the initial contract.

In addition to the horse show, extra attractions helped bring in new audiences during the week, build attendance and educate the public, reinforcing the mission of the show. For example, an educational Youth

Above: 1996 Cleveland Grand Prix winners Yankee Zulu and Todd Minikus. *Chagrin Valley PHA Horse Shows Inc*.

Right: Margie Goldstein, shown here aboard Pamina L, won her first Cleveland Grand Prix in 1992 and went on to set a record, winning it a total of ten times on a variety of horses. *Chagrin Valley PHA Horse Shows Inc*.

Day for groups such as summer camps and Saturday's Family Day, with children's games and entertainment, introduced more people to the horse show. Once visitors arrived, they found a boutique and treats area with food and shopping, as well as a friendly costume character mascot named Hunter the Horse and even a chance to take a behind-the-scenes tour of the horse show and stable area.

"We really try to have an intimate touchy-feely grounds set up so that people can interact and get close to the riders and horses," said Schneider. "Other shows don't let the public near the stable area or riders, but our grounds lend themselves to involvement and being a part of it all. At other shows, there is also so much hustle and bustle that it isn't exhibitor-friendly. We have a decent start and end time and go out of our way to keep that."

Exhibitors enjoyed the extra attractions, too. There were also exhibitor parties and a special hospitality tent with snacks from local restaurants; awards for best groom, stable tack room and sportsmanship; and even a special awards presentation for the best school horse from local riding stables.

The show had 60 ringside boxes available for purchase during the week, and on Sunday, it sold 150 boxes. The day of the Cleveland Grand Prix attracted large audiences, so there was no need to offer extra attractions. The show committee continued the tradition of grand prix festivities and exhibitions of dressage, carriages and the Chagrin Valley Hunt before the big event. It hired more off-duty police and Metroparks rangers to assist with crowd control and made provisions at nearby Orange High School to run a shuttle service when the extra parking lot became too full.

By all standards, the 1996 comeback was a success as an estimated twenty thousand spectators turned out and five hundred horses were entered in the show.

National Recognition

The national equestrian community recognized the Chagrin Valley PHA Horse Show and Cleveland Grand Prix comeback achievement as well. The popular equestrian publication *Spur: The Magazine of Equestrian and Country Life* named the KeyBank Hunter Jumper Classic to its list of the top ten equestrian events in a feature titled "Hot Tickets." According to the 1997 May/June issue of *Spur*, "Northeast Ohio is one of the horse world's lesser known treasures, but that makes it no less beautiful. It is the base for the

Chagrin Valley and Grand River Hunts and the home of many equestrians. A waterfall draws visitors to charming downtown Chagrin Falls, where the streets can be toured by horse-drawn carriage."

Other events on the list included the Devon Horse Show (Pennsylvania); the Pebble Beach Equestrian Classic (California); Long Island, New York's Hampton Classic; the Bayer/USET Festival of Champions in Gladstone, New Jersey; Lake Placid's I Love New York Horse Shows; the Pacific Classic in Del Mar, California; the Mercedes-Benz Gold Cup Final in Bridgehampton, New York; the Travers Stakes in Saratoga, New York; and Europe's Royal Pageant of the Horse in England.

Building on Success

With a stellar comeback year behind it, the CVPHA board worked to repeat the success and add attractions that would build attendance. The board

Organizers celebrate the comeback. *From left to right*: Betty Weibel, Chuck Kinney, Howard Lewis, Laddie Andahazy, Tom Visconsi Jr. and Karen Schneider. *Chagrin Valley PHA Horse Shows Inc.*

and its army of two hundred volunteers led by Chairman Karen Schneider were committed to growth. Leah Stroud remained on the board, and several others rotated as co-chairmen over the next decades: Tom Visconsi Jr., Betty Weibel, Chuck Kinney and Gail Tobin.

Organizers had approached the U.S. Dog Agility Association and invited it to share the Cleveland Metroparks Polo Field grounds and horse show amenities for its tenth annual Grand Prix of Dog Agility Championship. The canines drew large audiences of canine exhibitors and spectators, who could also watch the horse show for a single ticket price. The canine championship attracted more than three hundred highly trained dogs from more than thirty states and Canada, was televised on Animal Planet and garnered its own share of media coverage. The four-day event concluded in time for the $30,000 KeyBank Cleveland Grand Prix to begin, so there was no conflict with the star of the show. The relationship worked well and lasted many years.

In a display of creativity, organizers developed a unique event combining the canine agility and show jumping into a single event in the same ring. The $3,500 Dog and Horse Relay Race was a popular Friday evening attraction in the jumper ring and the first event of its kind in the United States.

The Dog and Horse Relay Race paired canine agility competitors with show jumpers; Tricia Booker demonstrates. *Chagrin Valley PHA Horse Shows Inc.*

However, the biggest draw of the show was, as always, the $30,000 Cleveland Grand Prix. After an all-night flight returning from a Hawaiian vacation, Margie Goldstein-Engle arrived in Ohio just hours before winning the coveted 1997 Cleveland title. She rode five of the seventeen grand prix starters, and the victory odds were in her favor. She won with Hidden Creek's Glory, a green horse she had been riding for less than six weeks, and this was their second grand prix appearance together. Pennsylvania's Cian McDermott and Catch the Wind had debuted on the grand prix circuit two weeks earlier and took home the red ribbon for second place, while Chuck Waters and Peace Pipe finished third, just ahead of defending champions Todd Minikus and Yankee Zulu. Nearly eight thousand people enjoyed the sunny afternoon and beautiful course designed by Jose Gamarra, a native of Bolivia.

Local landscapers had contributed their talents to decorating obstacles on the course and around the show grounds and received special recognition for their efforts. "Cleveland always has a great turnout. Fans in this area are very enthusiastic, which makes show jumping special for all of us riders. It helps add more excitement to our sport," said Goldstein-Engle.[69]

Goldstein-Engle defended her Cleveland Grand Prix title in 1998, but amateur rider Ellen Talbert of Cedarburg, Wisconsin, scored an upset win. Riding her own horse, Grand Jete, a French-bred Selle Français stallion, she topped the field of twenty-four. Talbert, who rode with Donald and Richard Cheska, had taken a spill in the first round aboard another horse but returned with Grand Jete to turn in a clean round.[70] Only five riders made it to the jump-off over the tough course designed by Jose Gamarra. Although she had four entries in the class, five-time AGA Rider of the Year Margie Goldstein-Engle didn't have a horse make the jump-off.

During the two years the Cleveland Grand Prix had been cancelled, it had lost its place on the American Grand Prix Association schedule and had to wait two years for an opening to arise before it could return as a tour stop. Although spectators continued to multiply in the stands, organizers were concerned that they needed to be a part of a grand prix series to give riders an added incentive to travel to the Chagrin Valley. They joined the National Grand Prix League; however, in 1998, Gene Mische helped the Cleveland Grand Prix rejoin the American Grand Prix Series.

With the AGA return came an abundance of colorful sponsor jumps, in addition to the local sponsor jumps such as the rainbow jump that had been added for the KeyBank Cleveland Grand Prix and presented by University Hospitals (Rainbow Babies and Children's Hospital). The AGA luxury car sponsors also added well-placed vehicles ringside and even inside the competition arena. Beyond the title sponsor, nearly all of the classes at the weeklong show were sponsored, and the support of cash or services ranged from the smaller individual level through the five-digit corporate level. It all added up to help the show's bottom line and get them on solid ground again.

Steve Stephens returned as course designer for the 1999 $35,000 KeyBank Cleveland Grand Prix, and the fences were set high in the first round at five feet with five-foot spreads. Goldstein-Engle was a top contender to regain her dominance in the Chagrin Valley with four of her five entries qualifying for the ten-horse jump-off. One of those horses was a new mount, and this was only her third grand prix with Adam. The pair was the last to go on course, topping the twenty-four starters and jump-off challengers to win. Although it was her third time winning the Cleveland Grand Prix, she was just getting started on her collection of Cleveland Grand Prix victories.

Chapter 10

THE NEW MILLENNIUM

Cleveland Grand Prix and Nonprofit Status Attract New Sponsors

According to the U.S. Equestrian Federation, there were 224 grand prix in the United States in 2000, and the Chagrin Valley PHA board was very experienced in handling sponsors now. It knew how to recruit and retain companies and planned ahead for KeyBank's exit. In 2000, the board welcomed a new title sponsor from the financial world, Merrill Lynch. The firm was attracted by the exciting sport of show jumping and the involvement of Northeast Ohio equestrians.

The 501(c)(3) horse show's voluntary board of trustees was composed of some prominent residents, business leaders and equestrians. The board and committee members oversaw such areas of responsibility as vendors, box seat sales, ribbon and trophy distribution, publicity, parking and permits, exhibitor hospitality and extra events such as Family and Youth Days. An additional volunteer team of about two hundred community members helped run the show in July and aided in grounds set up, staffing the box seat area, running special events and manning the welcome tent. The board recruited heavily from the equestrian community and established a system to train the workers before the show. It also provided logoed shirts and hats to wear on the job, as well as food and beverages to make the role appealing. Volunteers received tickets for friends and family to attend and were entered in a prize drawing for every shift worked. Many of the employed volunteers planned their vacation time from their work so they could participate in the event and enjoy the camaraderie.

In keeping with the new mission, proceeds from the show benefitted many local charities, including Fieldstone Farm Therapeutic Riding Center of Bainbridge Township, the primary beneficiary, which also shared its volunteer pool. Among the other organizations that benefited from the Classic were the Chagrin Falls Volunteer Fire Department, the Chagrin Valley Hunt, Cleveland Metroparks, the Cleveland Zoological Society, the Diabetes Association of Greater Cleveland, the Geauga Humane Society, the Ohio Horseman's Council, the United States Equestrian Team and the World Hunter Association.

The thirty-fifth anniversary of the nation's first grand prix had a number of celebrations planned around the $35,000 Merrill Lynch Cleveland Grand Prix. Merrill Lynch introduced new audiences to the horse show while promoting its involvement to their financial services clientele. The result was overwhelming, as the firm began receiving requests for tickets from out-of-state clients who wanted to enjoy the VIP chalet experience. A new permanent wood pavilion with concrete flooring, ceiling fans and lights was eventually constructed by the CVPHA to replace the chalet tent, which could get very hot in the summer. Fans from across Ohio as well as outside the state also filled the box seats and bleachers for the grand prix. More than forty thousand spectators passed through the gates during the weeklong event, breaking the previous year's attendance record.

Fieldstone Farm Therapeutic Riding Center held its annual Summer Fling benefit during the show. Despite torrential downpours accompanied by major thunderstorms, organizers of the benefit celebrated their biggest fundraising event in the center's twenty-two-year history, earning $73,000.

Competing Against Mother Nature

On Grand Prix Sunday, an overflowing crowd of ten thousand watched with anticipation as defending champion Margie Goldstein-Engle repeated her second straight win at the $35,000 Merrill Lynch Cleveland Grand Prix. She gave fans their money's worth, riding Hidden Creek's Laurel, an eleven-year-old Dutch jumper that was making a comeback after sustaining an injury in Europe the previous year. Although the inclement weather caused scratches from the original thirty-one entries due to the mud and boggy footing, twenty-five horses competed, with only three jumping clean in the first round. Jump-off contenders Candice King aboard Cinderella and Laura Kraut aboard Anthem both scored four faults, and Goldstein-Engle, the last to go in the tiebreaker, knew she only had to jump clean to win. Kraut and Goldstein-Engle shared another bond later that year as teammates (on different horses) at the Sydney Olympic Games, where they finished sixth.

This was Goldstein-Engle's fourth Cleveland Grand Prix victory, making her the all-time record holder. Until 2000, she had been tied with Rodney Jenkins with three. The sport's winningest equestrian held a number of records outside Cleveland, too: most AGA wins with the same horse in the same season (five wins on Saluut II in 1991), most grand prix wins in a single season (eleven) and two grand prix wins in two days. She was the first rider to place six horses in the ribbons in a single grand prix class and the first rider to ever win first through fifth place consecutively in a single grand prix class.

Todd Minikus, who won the 1996 Cleveland Grand Prix, had a fall in the first round in 2000, during which many riders struggled because of the wet footing. "The horses were sinking six inches, which added to the height of the fences. The course was deep, so it rode really big and the horses had to make a gigantic effort," he said.[71]

Course designer Steve Stephens admitted he wanted the Cleveland course to be challenging. "I built the course bigger than I might have for another $35,000 grand prix because this one is special. Not only was it the first in the nation, but it was the 35th anniversary."[72]

"It's fun to come back to Cleveland," said Stephens, the 1970 winner aboard Toy Soldier. "The Cleveland Grand Prix used to be the most prestigious grand prix on the tour." Stephens's last appearance in Cleveland as a rider was when he piloted the flamboyant stallion VIP to a clear round in the 1986 grand prix, and courses had changed considerably since he was competing. "In the early years, such as when I won the Cleveland Grand Prix, courses were very big, very large," he said. "They weren't necessarily technical, but in size, they were bigger than what we jump now." He explained that decades ago, fence building greatly contributed to the results a course designer would find at the end of the class, and he had to consider that factor when designing. The jump rails used to be much heavier, and jump cups (the metal or plastic holders that attach the rails to the jump standards) were deeper. Today, the rails are machine-rolled, lighter and very uniform, while a vast selection of jump cups are available from the same deep holders to those that are completely flat. (Plank fences, such as those that depict sponsors' names, are often set with flat cups to test a horse's carefulness.)[73]

2001 Cleveland Grand Prix winners Sundance Kid and Laura Chapot. *Chagrin Valley PHA Horse Shows Inc.*

Family was the theme of the 2001 $35,000 Merrill Lynch Cleveland Grand Prix, and it had a storybook ending for Laura Chapot and Cleveland fans. She became the third member of the Chapot family to capture the Cleveland Grand Prix, following her mother Mary's 1965 victory on Tomboy and her father Frank's win in 1971 on Grey Carrier. The twenty-eight-year-old rode a twelve-year-old speedy Dutch warmblood, Sundance Kid, to score her own Cleveland Grand Prix victory.

"It was neat to win here—not only because my mother won the first grand prix here but also because of all the people. The crowd is so enthusiastic and so great," said Chapot. "It is all about teamwork, and my mother was just as excited as I was." Her father called from Sweden, where he was traveling with the USET, to see how she had done.

Chapot and her mother/coach traveled from their home Neshanic Station, New Jersey, to Cleveland with five horses and no grooms. "Riding and competing has always been about family. Coming to the show was like a mini-vacation for us. It was nice to take care of all the horses ourselves," she said.[74]

There were twenty-two horses in the grand prix that day, and five made the jump-off. Two of them were ridden by the husband-and-wife duo of

Awards presentation with Laura and mother, Mary Chapot, representatives of Merrill Lynch. *Chagrin Valley PHA Horse Shows Inc.*

David and Laura Steffee. Laura went early in the jump-off aboard Perle and had the lead with a fast clean round until she was beat by Chapot and settled for second place. David jumped-off with Luna but scored six penalties for having a rail down and time faults. Third place went to the 1989 Cleveland Grand Prix winner Donald Cheska, riding Jubulent.

The event was particularly special and sentimental for the Steffees, who had originally met at the horse show years before and eventually married. David grew up riding in the Chagrin Valley. "I grew up working and learning to ride on this field, so to be able to make the jump-off and be in the finals is something I will always remember," he said. "I'm on top of the world after the way things finished up this week."[75]

Laura Steffee had returned to the saddle after recovering from a broken back, which made her finish even more special. Perle was jointly owned by Sierra del Sol and Craighead Farm, a Novelty, Ohio breeding farm owned by David Steffee's mother, Billie, a longtime Chagrin Valley horse show sponsor and board member.

Funding from Merrill Lynch helped elevate the Cleveland Grand Prix to $40,000 in 2002, and Candice King of Wellington, Florida, took home more than her share of the purse. She made a clean sweep, finishing first aboard Espadon, second aboard Camillo, third with Elu de la Hardiere and fourth with Gosse D'Orion. In the field of thirty-two horses, the only other rider to jump fault-free was Laura Steffee aboard Perle, and they finished fifth. "Because I'm riding for three different owners, I had to try to win with each horse even though I knew I had already won," King said after the event.[76]

In 2003, Margie Engle returned to the winner's circle at the $40,000 Merrill Lynch Cleveland Grand Prix aboard the twelve-year-old stallion Julius. The horse had been competing in the amateur jumpers prior to the grand prix win. Lisa Jacquin rode Justice to finish second, and Laura Steffee rode Perle to finish third. Once again, the horse show was hampered by poor weather as torrential rain and flooding nearly shut down the competition. The all-weather hunter rings proved valuable, allowing the jumper competition to go by moving off the grass. The greatest damage that year was in the Cleveland Metroparks South Reservation's South Field, where tents had been set up for stabling. Flooding created deep mud and washed out the roads, making conditions unbearable.

Immediately following the show, the Chagrin Valley PHA's board of directors committed to costly permanent grounds improvements with a $50,000 pledge of support in the form of a loan from the Billie Steffee Family Fund of the Cleveland Foundation. The excavation and restoration work included rebuilding roads and other renovations to the competition and spectator areas. In 2005, the CVPHA received another major loan from Steffee and an investment in the grounds to install a state-of-the-art footing system that included a computer system to monitor moisture and adjust drainage as needed. According to Schneider, the ring system and footing were selected after seeing how well they performed in the international ring at a Wellington, Florida horse show site. The new two-hundred- by three-hundred-foot ring and drainage system was installed in time for the fortieth anniversary celebration of the Cleveland Grand Prix, replacing the grass footing but allowing the show to remain on the historic grounds of the first grand prix in the Western Hemisphere.

Olympic veteran Margie Engle entered the record books by winning the 2004 $40,000 Merrill Lynch Cleveland Grand Prix for an unprecedented sixth time, riding Hidden Creek's chestnut gelding Wapino. Over the years, Engle brought numerous young horses and seasoned entries to Cleveland as she built her grand prix string, and she considered Wapino to be one of her most talented mounts.

Three-time Cleveland Grand Prix winners Wapino and Margie Goldstein-Engle. *Chagrin Valley PHA Horse Shows Inc.*

The following year, a capacity crowd was on hand to celebrate the fortieth anniversary of the Cleveland Grand Prix and see defending champs Engle and Wapino win again. It was the forty-seven-year-old rider's third consecutive Cleveland win. True to form, Mother Nature played a role in the event, but the wet weather didn't hamper the competition that year because of the investment in the new ring. "Considering the weather, the footing held up fantastically. The effort they made to put in a new surface this year was great. Without [the new surface], there's no way we could have competed today without jeopardizing the welfare of the horses," said Engle, who received $12,000 for the win. Candice King and Camillo challenged but had to settle for second place and the $8,000 check.[77]

Engle continued her streak, winning the 2006 $65,000 Merrill Lynch Cleveland Grand Prix an unprecedented third consecutive time on the same horse. Her biggest challenger that year was McLain Ward, of Brewster, New York, who had a faster jump-off time but a rail down at the last obstacle. An aggressive rider with a strong will to win, Engle was a crowd-pleaser in the jump-off. She told reporters after the record win, "I really enjoy this show,

2007 Cleveland Grand Prix winners Nerina and Kent Farrington. *Chagrin Valley PHA Horse Shows Inc.*

and I enjoy coming here. This show always draws a great enthusiastic crowd, and it is inspiring. It motivates me when I'm in the ring."

It looked like Engle and Wapino would go on to international success after Cleveland, but tragedy struck in 2007 when Wapino died of complications from colic surgery. The loss was devastating for Engle and owner Mike Polaski, who had high hopes for the twelve-year-old horse.

The following July, when twenty-six-year-old Kent Farrington arrived in Cleveland for the 2007 $50,000 Cleveland Grand Prix, he had been on a winning streak since April, claiming six grand prix aboard Up Chiqui. But his winning streak with Up Chiqui ended in Cleveland when he knocked down two rails in the first round for eight faults. However, Farrington made the seven-horse jump-off aboard Nerina, a horse he had been riding for only a month and a half. He went as fast as he could on the twelve-year-old Dutch mare, knowing his toughest challenger, Margie Engle, was behind him in the tiebreaker on Hidden Creek's Calippo. Farrington's time was two seconds faster, and Engle settled for second place.

However, Engle returned in 2008 to reclaim her Cleveland prominence and the blue ribbon as she was back in the Cleveland Grand Prix winner's circle. She claimed the win aboard Hidden Creek's Pamina L, a new grey

2011 Cleveland Grand Prix winners Toronto and Candice King. *Chagrin Valley PHA Horse Shows Inc.*

horse that had been imported earlier in the year from Germany, where she had shown in lower jumper classes and been a broodmare.

In 2009, the $35,000 Cleveland Grand Prix had its smallest field: twelve starters. Wisconsin pro Robert Kraut scored an upset win, riding Happy Hill Farm's Accordian to the horse's first grand prix victory. They were one of four in the jump-off. The favorite, Margie Engle, failed to score a faultless round on her three horses and did not earn a trip to the jump-off. Johnstown, Ohio's Angela Klein-Moore rode Claus to a second-place finish.

True to form, Engle returned in 2010 to win the Cleveland Grand Prix for her tenth time aboard Indigo, and she finished second riding Hidden Creek's Pamina L. Although the horse show now spanned three weeks to attract riders by reducing travel costs between shows, the Cleveland Grand Prix was still the highlight of the Hunter/Jumper Classic, which drew twenty thousand to twenty-five thousand fans overall. Among the competitors were former winner Debbie Shaffner Stephens and Olympic gold medalist Joe Fargis, still in pursuit of his first Cleveland Grand Prix win.

Veteran professional rider Candice King returned to claim her second blue ribbon in the 2011 $30,000 Cleveland Grand Prix. Riding Toronto, an eleven-year-old horse that entertained fans with his bucking between jumps, King bested a field of nineteen horses and six in the jump-off to take home the $9,000 first-prize check. Her closest challenger was seventeen-year-old Shawn Casady of Midtown, Tennessee, aboard Skara Glen's Basel. Doug Russell of Ocala, Florida, was the course designer and had built a challenging course, but only two horses were fault-free in the jump-off, separated by just hundredths of a second. King crossed the timers in 39.606 seconds, and Casady's time was 39.623.

Chapter 11

The American Gold Cup Returns to Cleveland

It had been ten years since Stadium Jumping had managed a horse show in Cleveland at the Metroparks Polo Field, and Michael Morrissey Jr. had taken the helm of the Florida company. The nephew of Gene Mische, Morrissey was a seasoned and respected horse show manager when he returned to the Chagrin Valley with a unique idea. His vision was to bring the American Gold Cup back to its 1970 Cleveland birthplace, the Cleveland Metroparks Polo Field. Many of the members of the Morrissey family still lived here; there was a strong attachment to the area, and Mische was supportive of the idea. However, instead of a July show, the event would now take place in September.

Morrissey approached Karen Schneider, chairwoman of the Chagrin Valley PHA Horse Show, to share his vision of how that the move would benefit both shows. They met to work out details on how the two show jumping events could work together. Schneider provided information on how the CVPHA set up its horse show at the Polo Field, as well as information on vendors and community connections. Morrissey pledged use of the Stadium Jumping–owned equipment, including chalet tenting, box seats and show grounds tents, tables and chairs, as well as fencing and manpower resources. They explored ways to co-promote their events and made sure they would not approach sponsors that were already committed, leaving no possibility of compromising their supporters.

Morrissey recalled:

The Gold Cup had a great run at Devon, and it was sad to leave that historic show grounds, but we moved to another historic grounds and took the American

The American Gold Cup setup and new arena footing gave the show grounds a face-lift. *Ohio Photographers*.

Gold Cup back to where it began 36 years ago. The first American Gold Cup was held in conjunction with the Chagrin Valley PHA Horse Show, in 1970, at the historic Polo Field, site of the nation's first show jumping grand prix. Then the Gold Cup moved to Florida and became the forerunner of today's American Invitational in Tampa. It later moved to Philadelphia, where it remained for 27 years. With the installation of a new international show ring on the Metroparks Polo Field in 2005, the grounds met international standards for competitions such as the Gold Cup.[78]

Schneider had the following to say about the partnership:

We are happy to welcome the American Gold Cup back to Northeast Ohio. These equestrian events will complement each other because they are two very different types of events. The Chagrin show offers over one hundred classes for beginner through the Cleveland Grand Prix over the course of eight days in July, while the Gold Cup focuses on less than 30 exclusive jumper classes. This is a coup for Northeast Ohio! Many of the staff and volunteers who work the Chagrin Valley Horse Show are lending a hand to help the Gold Cup be a success.[79]

2006 American Gold Cup winners Vegas and Christine McCrea, Marc Beshany and Michael Morrissey. *Ohio Photographers.*

In 2006, the Chagrin Valley PHA Horse Show and the Cleveland Grand Prix were sponsored by Merrill Lynch. Morrissey was able to secure title sponsor funding for the Gold Cup from another prominent financial services firm, and in the fall, he hosted the Wachovia Securities American Gold Cup with a $100,000 finale. The main event was won by Vegas, a twelve-year-old stallion ridden by Christine McCrae. The nation's top riders and some international stars were attracted by the prize money and international FEI World Cup qualifying status. Stadium Jumping showed its talent in staging the grounds with a new approach around the new show jumping arena. Morrissey brought in aerial lifts for lighting the evening classes and enclosed the international jumper arena with seating to create an intimate setting. Even the warm-up area and in-gate were rearranged from the traditional July set up to make use of the all-weather hunter rings and efficient access. Morrissey said:

> *There is a very strong equestrian community in the Chagrin Valley, and they embraced the show, bringing in some local entries and many spectators. Wachovia Securities' Northeast Ohio leader, Marc Beshany, and his*

management team supported us as our title sponsor as we reintroduced the show in Cleveland, and they were a fantastic sponsor.[80]

It was a strong strategic move for two of the nation's top horse show jumping events to team up to promote grand prix show jumping in Cleveland in 2006. Organizers of the Cleveland Grand Prix and the American Gold Cup took it a step further when they established a $50,000 challenge to encourage the world's best grand prix riders to travel to Northeast Ohio. They announced in 2007 that any rider who won both the $50,000 Cleveland Grand Prix in July and the $100,000 American Gold Cup in September in the same year with the same horse would be awarded a $50,000 bonus.[81]

Schneider noted, "Our return to Cleveland last year was a tremendous success. Riders love this venue, and they love the community support they get when they return to Cleveland each year. Our hope is that this incentive will bring even more world-class competitors to Northeast Ohio each summer."

During the 2007 summer Chagrin Valley horse show, Merrill Lynch's sponsorship came to a close. However, the 2007 $30,000 Cleveland Grand Prix attracted a broad range of riders who were also competing for a special bonus opportunity. The bonus was an incentive to many riders to attend the Cleveland Grand Prix, but only the winners, Nerina and Kent Farrington, emerged as bonus contenders. Mario Deslauriers dashed Farrington's hopes, though, when he rode Paradigm to win the 2007 American Gold Cup, and no one claimed the $50,000 bonus.

The Wachovia Securities American Gold Cup was a hit in Cleveland with fans and riders. After the exciting 2008 class was won by Norman Dello Joio aboard Malcolm, the event ran into organizational issues that halted future plans. The Cleveland Grand Prix was once again the Chagrin Valley's solo show jumping attraction.

The Changing Grand Prix Circuit

The equestrian world was changing, and for the organizers behind the scenes, show jumping was as competitive an environment as it was for the riders in the show ring. By 2007, there was a total of 358 grand prix in the United States, according to the U.S. Equestrian Federation. The number of sanctioned hunter/jumper competitions had reached 1,520, ranging from local-level horse shows to top-rated AA horse shows offering the highest prize money—and many of those top-rated shows offered a grand prix. Riders had more options, so the prize purses needed to be competitive to attract the most popular horses and riders.

The American Grand Prix Association, which was founded in 1978, presented its final Rider, Horse and Rookie of the Year Awards in 2007, and the series quietly ceased. The AGA's main emphasis was organizing the highest echelon of the sport; as a result, the level of competition in the United States advanced dramatically, and the sport became a viable marketing alternative for corporate sponsors.[82]

Formally initiated thirteen years after the first Cleveland Grand Prix was held in 1965, the AGA began with sixteen grand prix on the 1978 tour, including the Cleveland Grand Prix. The average event purse in 1978 was $15,400, which was multiplied far beyond expectations, thanks to the support of such sponsors as Mercedes-Benz of North America, Anheuser-Busch, Rolex Watch USA and more. Many of the national tour sponsors continued to be involved in show jumping events on a local or regional sponsorship basis. The American Grand Prix Association had achieved all of its goals for the sport.

Chapter 12

A FOGGY FUTURE

The year 2015 marks the fiftieth anniversary of grand prix show jumping in America, and it all began right here in Cleveland. The Cleveland Grand Prix is a legacy that has been passed on from generation to generation of horse show lovers and people who share a deep love and passion for horses and the experiences that they bring to our lives. It is more than just a show; it reinforces Cleveland's place in the equine world and brings people together from near and far to share in a tradition. This show's survival, like all great institutions, is dependent on continued good stewardship. We hope that the equine community's current and future generations will share in our passion and efforts to keep the show thriving.
—Karen Schneider

In 2012, the Chagrin Valley PHA Horse Show proceeded, despite a lack of title sponsor funding, because there were many local supporters. The American Grand Prix sponsorships and television coverage of the past had ceased. Within the industry, the number of horse shows with grand prix finales had grown steadily, giving exhibitors many options. A number of shows had expanded to multi-week schedules and installed permanent facilities. Horse shows in Florida and Kentucky, for example, were held at venues with permanent stables, turnout paddocks and added amenities. This was in stark contrast to the tented stalls and temporary facilities at the Cleveland Metroparks Polo Field show grounds. Horse shows had become competitive, and even some local trainers and riders in Ohio were heading out of town in July instead of supporting the Chagrin Valley PHA show on home turf.

The Chagrin Valley PHA board and committees worked hard so the show could go on, and show jumping fans in 2012 were treated to a down-to-the-wire finish when a new name was engraved on the Grand Prix record. Federico Sztyrle and Crossfire 10, a ten-year-old Holsteiner gelding, won the $30,000 Cleveland Grand Prix during their first visit to the Chagrin Valley. Born and raised in Argentina, Sztyrle, forty-seven, had been living in the United States for sixteen years and was based in Wellington, Florida.

The Cleveland Grand Prix had a diverse field of twenty-four horses composed of both international and local competitors, including Olympian Joe Fargis, Venezuela's Pablo Barrios and local professional Megan Moshontz-Bash. Longtime course designer Steve Stephens had returned and built a technically demanding course. "[It is] exactly the kind of course you would expect from the man who designed the Olympic courses in Beijing. It's so exciting to have such amazing talent—course designers, riders, horses—right here in Cleveland's backyard," said Bash.

Sztyrle and Crossfire finished the jump-off on top with a time of 40.183—more than one second faster than Venezuelan Juan Ortiz and Accordance, who took second place. Rebecca Conway of Salt Lake City, Utah, and Twister finished third. A downpour during the pre-event festivities heavily soaked the grand prix ring, but the advanced drainage system worked well to remove the water that covered the arena. "The ring is amazing," said Sztyrle. "I really like this show, and I plan to return next year. This show is lucky [for me]."[83]

Debating the Future

After the 2012 show concluded, the board met to discuss the future, and serious consideration was devoted to the topic of whether the show should go on.

Overseeing the horse show and its $800,000 budget was not an easy task. Some of the largest expenses were allocated to stabling and grounds equipment such as tents, bleachers and restrooms ($243,000); overall manpower, including officials (judges, course designers, stewards) and crew, hotels and expenses ($220,000); and prize money expenditures ($170,000). Income was generated from sponsorships, entry fees, general admission and box seat sales, as well as vendor fees.

The financial report for 2012 revealed the horse show had its best year for entries; however, it didn't make a profit. According to Schneider, the horse show itself was successful, but necessary capital improvement expenditures for water pressure additions totaled $25,000 and put the organization in the red. Sponsorship was another concern because although there were loyal sponsors like generous Billie Steffee, there was not a wide range of sponsors or major corporate backing to fund the large-purse events, particularly the Cleveland Grand Prix. Another area of strong concern was a lack of new volunteers willing to step up and take over the leadership roles on committees and the board. Although the organization carried the CVPHA initials in its name for Professional Horsemen's Association, there were actually very few professionals who earned their living in the equestrian world on the board of trustees.

Karen Schneider said:

> *Over the years, many board members have donated money or put in countless hours working the show before, during and after the event...others donated services like landscaping, automobile loans or office staff. It's time for the next generation to step up, and we don't see anyone in sight, so that is a concern. I would hate to see the show go downhill for lack of interest, but our generation is going out, and the new one should be coming in. We are between generations and haven't found the next team to take over...we are aging out, and people are leaving and retiring like they did when Leah Stroud and Stan Stone were co-chairs.*

As board members discussed options for the future, they considered all the possibilities. Should they end the horse show and Cleveland Grand Prix and go out on a high note before they reach the fifty-year milestone? Or should they take a year off and try to rebuild and reinvigorate the board, committees and sponsors?

When 2013 arrived, the Chagrin Valley PHA Horse Show and $30,000 Cleveland Grand Prix were still in business and on the competition calendar.

The Cleveland Grand Prix continued the traditional pre-event festivities that had preceded every grand prix since the first one in 1965. The Chagrin Valley Hunt made an appearance for the crowd, which numbered well over five thousand fans. Dressage, a carriage with officials and the Cleveland Metroparks Color Guard set the stage for the main event.

The 2013 $30,000 Cleveland Grand Prix crowned nineteen-year-old Shawn Casady champion aboard Twister and gave fans an exciting finish. Casady topped a field of sixteen horses with five in the jump-off, finishing in 38.978—ahead of sixty-five-year-old Olympian Joe Fargis, who was riding

134

2013 Cleveland Grand Prix winners Twister and nineteen-year-old Shawn Casady. *Chagrin Valley PHA Horse Shows Inc.*

Lariat and finished in second place with a time of 39.171. Richard Cheska and Quick Tempo finished third. The crowd was treated to an exciting tie-breaking round as each horse that entered the ring to jump-off took over the lead. Fargis had been competing in the Cleveland Grand Prix for decades and complimented the event, "Every jump was its own challenge. Everything was well done—the footing, the course, everything."[84]

Giving Back to the Community

At a time when organizers could have been meeting to plan a fifty-year Cleveland Grand Prix celebration to recognize the first show jumping grand prix in North America, they made the decision to cancel the 2014 event.

New competition schedule changes on the circuit outside Ohio had created a domino effect of conflicts that threatened to deter riders from Cleveland, and it was one more issue to add to a growing list of challenges. Show manager Ralph Alfano, who had been with the event since 2005, and consultant Michael Morrissey supported the decision to put the show on hold for a year.

Earlier in the year, the board lost its co-chairman, Chuck Kinney, who died soon after board member and former co-chairman Howard Lewis had passed away. Both men had contributed their time and talents to the Chagrin Valley PHA Horse Show for decades and had been a part of the Cleveland Grand Prix history. The board hoped that a year off would produce new leaders, sponsors and supporters to carry on the tradition of the Chagrin Valley.

Since the earliest rainy competitions on the Cleveland Metroparks Polo Field, the Chagrin Valley PHA Horse Show had worked to improve the facility it leased, and many of the improvements were enjoyed by other organizations and Cleveland Metroparks users year-round. Over the years, the CVPHA had funded well over $500,000 in improvements, including landscaping, drainage upgrades, a city water pipeline, rings and fencing, box seat roofing, an announcer stand/storage garage, an entrance gazebo and two permanent pavilions.

During the horse show's history, more than $1 million had been raised for charities by the Chagrin Valley PHA Horse Show Inc. In addition to creating an incredible equestrian sport, the board had created a legacy of giving back to the community.[85]

Maureen Foster, development director for Fieldstone Farm Therapeutic Riding Center, said:

> *The horse show was instrumental in helping Fieldstone Farm TRC reach its many goals. The financial support has greatly impacted the quality of riding lessons provided to our over 700 students annually. Many students who cannot afford the full lesson fee have been able to ride because of the assistance of such donors as the Classic. This event has also provided a tremendous amount of publicity for our program, which has been wonderfully successful in recruiting more supporters, volunteers, horse donors, and students. Additionally, the annual competition for riders with disabilities has allowed our students the opportunity to showcase their riding talents to the diverse audience at the show.*[86]

The Cleveland Grand Prix contributed beyond its fundraising mission. The exciting visitor attraction had become an important destination with an economic impact that reached deep into Chagrin Valley businesses and Northeast Ohio's annual tourism trade.

The equestrian tradition in the Chagrin Valley attracted countless horsemen to compete and many more fans to enjoy the performances at the Cleveland Grand Prix. The sport is ingrained in the culture of the community and an important part of the heritage.

Leaving a Mark on History

If ever the sounds of hoof beats are silenced at the Chagrin Valley's Cleveland Metroparks Polo Field, the memory of the Cleveland Grand Prix will remain. Visitors to the Polo Field will see a permanent reminder of the equestrian legacy. In 2003, the historic significance of the Cleveland Grand Prix was recognized with the dedication of a bronze marker. A news release to media helped put the Cleveland Grand Prix in perspective with other Ohio sport contributions. It stated:

> *Ohio is well known for its contributions to the world of sports. It is home to the nation's first professional baseball team, the Cincinnati Reds; the birthplace of Olympian Jesse Owens and baseball's Cy Young; and home*

to the famous Soapbox Derby. But did you know that Ohio is also the birthplace of horse show jumping in North America?

To help honor this momentous sports achievement, the Ohio Bicentennial Commission (OBC) and the Chagrin Valley PHA Horse Show Inc. dedicated a bronze historical marker on the site of the first Cleveland Grand Prix in June 2003. Many Ohio sports achievements and legends were honored across the state with Ohio Bicentennial sports markers that June and highlighted during a special two-week sports period:

Jesse Owens, Olympian, Columbus
Cincinnati Reds, baseball, Cincinnati
Cy Young, baseball, Newcomerstown
Paul Brown/Cleveland Browns, Cleveland
Woody Hayes/Ohio Stadium, Columbus
Fleet Walker, baseball, Toledo
Soapbox Derby, Akron

The Ohio Bicentennial Commission's bronze historical marker honors the Cleveland Grand Prix. *Chagrin Valley PHA Horse Shows Inc.*

Dempsey-Willard fight, Toledo
Jack Kidwell, golf course designer, Dublin
Cleveland Grand Prix, horse show jumping, Moreland Hills[87]

Visitors to the Cleveland Metroparks Polo Field can see the bronze Ohio history marker on permanent display near the Route 87 entrance. It reads:

> *On July 22, 1965, nearly 10,000 spectators traveled to the Cleveland Metroparks Polo Field to witness the first-ever North American show jumping grand prix—the Cleveland Grand Prix. The event gave birth to the multimillion-dollar sport of grand prix show jumping in the United States. Held on the final day of the Chagrin Valley PHA Horse Show, the Cleveland Grand Prix was defined by a 844-yard course of 16 obstacles designed by Laddie Andahazy and D. Jerry Baker. Twenty riders from six countries—the United States, Canada, Mexico, France, Great Britain and Germany—competed over the course. Mary Mairs Chapot won the event on her horse Tomboy and her husband, Frank, an Olympic veteran, finished second aboard Manon.*

Appendix A

CLEVELAND GRAND PRIX
WINNERS

Year	Horse	Owner(s)	Rider
1965	Tomboy	Mary Chapot	Mary Chapot
1966	Silver Lining	Country Club Stable	Carlene Blunt
1967	Gustavus	Harry Gill	Rodney Jenkins
1968	Canadian Club	Ernest Samuel	Jim Day
1969	Lights Out	J. Moffat Dunlap	J. Moffat Dunlap
1970	Toy Soldier	Mrs. R.J. Reynolds	Steve Stephens
1971	Grey Carrier	Sandrellan Stable	Frank Chapot
1972	Rosie Report	J. Basil Ward	Michael Matz
1973	Springdale	Michael Cody	Bernie Traurig
1974	Coming Attraction	Friendship Farm	Thom Hardy
1975	Sandsablaze	Derby Hill Farm	Buddy Brown
1976	Balbuco	Mr. and Mrs. Patrick Butler	Conrad Homfeld
1977	Idle Dice	Harry Gill	Rodney Jenkins
1978	The Cardinal	Mr. and Mrs. E.R. Ismond	Bernie Traurig
1979	Second Balcony	Edie Spruance	Rodney Jenkins
1980	Abdullah	Williamsburg Farm	Debbie Shaffner
1981	Jet Run	F. Eugene Dixon	Michael Matz

Year	Horse	Owner(s)	Rider
1982	Noren	Plain Bay Farm Ltd.	Katie Monahan
1983	Jethro	Joe Wyant	Katie Monahan
1984	Brussels	Hunterdon Inc.	George Morris
1985	Corsair	Mrs. Betty Maniatty	Norman Dello Joio
1986	Albany	Sagamore Farm	Debbie Dolan
1987	Gem Twist	Michael Golden	Greg Best
1988	Northern Magic	Fisher & Oak Creek Farm	Beezie Patton
1989	Dury Lad	Mr. and Mrs. William Van Dyke	Donald Cheska
1990	Boysie II	Rita Curcio	James Young
1991	Oxo	Ri-Arm Farm	Peter Leone
1992	Daydream	DayDream Association	Margie Goldstein
1993	Samsung Woodstock	K.H. Lee and Chung L. Park	Susie Hutchison
1994–95	NOT HELD	N/A	N/A
1996	Yankee Zulu	YZ Partners	Todd Minikus
1997	Hidden Creek's Glory	Hidden Creek Farm	Margie Goldstein-Engle
1998	Grand Jete	Ellen Talbert	Ellen Talbert
1999	Adam	Lea Allen	Margie Goldstein-Engle
2000	Hidden Creek's Laurel	Hidden Creek Farm	Margie Goldstein-Engle
2001	Sundance Kid	Sundance Group	Laura Chapot
2002	Espadon	J. Peter Nissen	Candice King
2003	Julius	Daybreak Farm	Margie Engle
2004	Hidden Creek's Wapino	Hidden Creek Farm	Margie Engle
2005	Hidden Creek's Wapino	Hidden Creek Farm	Margie Engle
2006	Hidden Creek's Wapino	Hidden Creek Farm	Margie Engle
2007	Nerina	Javier Salvador	Kent Farrington
2008	Hidden Creek's Pamina L	Hidden Creek Farm	Margie Engle
2009	Accordian	Happy Hill Farm	Robert Kraut

CLEVELAND GRAND PRIX WINNERS

Year	Horse	Owner(s)	Rider
2010	Indigo	Gladewinds	Margie Engle
2011	Toronto	AAA Equestrian	Candice King
2012	Crossfire 10	Crossfire LLC	Federico Sztyrle
2013	Twister	Cavallo Farms LLC	Shawn Casady
2014	NOT HELD	N/A	N/A

Appendix B

U.S. OLYMPIC EQUESTRIAN TEAM MEMBERS—SHOW JUMPING

Year	Location	Team/Individual	Rider	Horse	Place
1912	Stockholm, Sweden	Team	Lieutenant Benjamin Lear	Poppy	Fourth
			Captain Guy Henry	Connie	
			Lieutenant John Montgomery	Deceive	
1920	Antwerp, Belgium	Individual	Major Henry Allen	Don	
			Major John Downer	Dick	
			Major William West	Prince	
		Team	Captain Harry Chamberlin	Nigra	Fifth
			Captain Karl Greenwald	Moses	
			Captain Vincent Erwin	Joffre	
			Major Sloan Doak	Rabbit Red	

Year	Location	Team/Individual	Rider	Horse	Place
1924	Paris, France	Team	Major John Barry	Nigra	Eliminated
			Major Sloan Doak	Joffre	
			Captain Vernon Padget	Little Canada	
			Lieutenant Frederic Bontecou	Bally McShane	
1928	Amsterdam, Holland	Team	Major Harry Chamberlin	Nigra	Ninth
			Captain Frank Carr	Proctor	
			Captain Adolphus Roffe	Fairfax	
1932	Los Angeles, United States	Individual	Major Harry Chamberlin	Show Girl	Second
		Team	Major Harry Chamberlin	Show Girl	Eliminated
			Captain William Bradford	Joe Aleshire	
			Lieutenant John Wofford	Babe Wartham	
1936	Berlin, Germany	Team	Captain Carl Raguse	Dakota	Fourth
			Major William Bradford	Don	
			Captain Cornelius Jadwin	Ugly	
1948	London, England	Team	Colonel Franklin Wing	Democrat	Eliminated
			Captain John Russell	Air Mail	
			Colonel Andrew Frierson	Rascal	
1952	Helsinki, Finland	Team	William Steinkraus	Hollandia	Bronze Medal
			Arthur McCashin	Miss Budweiser	
			John Russell	Democrat	

Year	Location	Team/ Individual	Rider	Horse	Place
1956	Stockholm, Sweden	Team	Hugh Wiley	Trail Guide	Fifth
			William Steinkraus	Night Owl	
			Frank Chapot	Belair	
1960	Rome, Italy	Individual	George Morris	Sinjon	
			Hugh Wiley	Master William	
			William Steinkraus	Riviera Wonder	
		Team	George Morris	Sinjon	Silver Medal
			Frank Chapot	Trail Guide	
			William Steinkraus	Ksard'Esprit	
1964	Tokyo, Japan	Team	Frank Chapot	San Lucas	Sixth
			Kathy Kusner	Untouchable	
			Mary Mairs	Tomboy	
1968	Mexico City, Mexico	Individual	William Steinkraus	Snowbound	First
			Frank Chapot	San Lucas	
			Kathy Kusner	Untouchable	
		Team	Mary Chapot	White Lightning	Fourth
			Kathy Kusner	Untouchable	
			Frank Chapot	San Lucas	
1972	Munich, West Germany	Individual	Neal Shapiro	Sloopy	Third
			Kathy Kusner	Fleet Apple	
			William Steinkraus	Snowbound	
		Team	Neal Shapiro	Sloopy	Silver Medal
			Kathy Kusner	Fleet Apple	
			Frank Chapot	White Lightning	
			William Steinkraus	Main Spring	

Year	Location	Team/ Individual	Rider	Horse	Place
1976	Montreal, Canada	Individual	Frank Chapot	Viscount	
			Dennis Murphy	Do Right	
			Buddy Brown	A Little Bit	
		Team	Buddy Brown	Sandsablaze	Fourth
			Robert Ridland	South Side	
			Michael Matz	Grande	
			Frank Chapot	Viscount	
1980	Alternate Olympics – Rotterdam, Holland	Individual	Melanie Smith	Calypso	Third
			Terry Rudd	Semi Tough	
			Norman Dello Joio	Allegro	
		Team	Katie Monahan	Silver Exchange	Fifth
			Norman Dello Joio	Allegro	
			Terry Rudd	Semi Tough	
			Melanie Smith	Calypso	
1984	Los Angeles, United States	Individual	Joe Fargis	Touch of Class	First
			Conrad Homfeld	Abdullah	Second
			Melanie Smith	Calypso	
		Team	Joe Fargis	Touch of Class	Gold Medal
			Leslie Burr	Albany	
			Conrad Homfeld	Abdullah	
			Melanie Smith	Calypso	
1988	Seoul, South Korea	Individual	Greg Best	Gem Twist	Second
		Team	Greg Best	Gem Twist	Silver Medal
			Anne Kursinski	Starman	
			Joe Fargis	Mill Pearl	
			Lisa Jacquin	For The Moment	
1992	Barcelona, Spain	Individual	Norman Dello Joio	Irish	Third
		Team	Norman Dello Joio	Irish	Fifth
			Lisa Jacquin	For The Moment	
			Anne Kursinski	Cannonball	
			Michael Matz	Heisman	

Year	Location	Team/Individual	Rider	Horse	Place
1996	Atlanta, United States	Team	Peter Leone	Legato	Silver Medal
			Leslie Burr Howard	Extreme	
			Anne Kursinski	Eros	
			Michael Matz	Rhum IV	
2000	Sydney, Australia	Team	Laura Kraut	Liberty	Sixth
			Lauren Hough	Clasiko	
			Nona Garson	Rhythmical	
			Margie Goldstein-Engle	Hidden Creek's Perin	
2004	Athens, Greece	Individual	Chris Kappler	Royal Kaliber	Second
		Team	Chris Kappler	Royal Kaliber	Gold Medal
			Beezie Madden	Authentic	
			Peter Wylde	Fein Cera	
			McLain Ward	Sapphire	
2008	Hong Kong, China	Individual	Beezie Madden	Authentic	Third
		Team	Laura Kraut	Cedric	Gold Medal
			Beezie Madden	Authentic	
			Will Simpson	CarlssonVomDach	
			McLain Ward	Sapphire	
2012	London, England	Team	Rich Fellers	Flexible	Sixth
			McLain Ward	Antares F	
			Beezie Madden	Via Volo	
			Reed Kessler	Cylana	

Appendix C

AMERICAN GRAND PRIX
ASSOCIATION HORSE OF THE YEAR

Year	Horse	Owner(s)
1978	Val De Loire	Stillmeadow Farm
1979	Balbuco	Mr. and Mrs. Patrick Butler
1980	Balbuco	Mr. and Mrs. Patrick Butler
1981	Jet Run	Mr. F. Eugene Dixon Jr.
1982	Noren	Plain Bay Farm
1983	Albany	Debbie Dolan and Sagamore Farm
1984	Albany	Debbie Dolan and Sagamore Farm
1985	The Governor	Mrs. W. Averell Harriman
1986	Sedac	Barney Ward
1987	Gem Twist	Michael Golden
1988	Special Envoy	Mrs. W. Averell Harriman
1989	Gem Twist	Michael Golden
1990	Lego	Prestige Properties
1991	For The Moment	BDJ Enterprises
1992	Budweiser Gem Twist	Michael Golden
1993	Denizen	USA Mobil and Elan Farm
1994	For The Moment	BDJ Enterprises
1995	Seven Wonder	Marley Goodman and Turtle Lane Farm

Year	Horse	Owner(s)
1996	Hidden Creek's Alvaretto	Hidden Creek Farm
1997	Dynamite	Alan Shore Jr.
1998	Twist du Valon	McLain Ward and Harry R. Gill
1999	Bellandonna	Plain Bay Farm
2000	Kroon Gravin	Sandra O'Donnell
2001	Viktor	McLain Ward and Harry R. Gill
2002	Royal Kaliber	Kamine family and Chris Kappler
2003	Hidden Creek's Jones	Hidden Creek Farm
2004	Glasgow	The Glasgow Group
2005	Madison	Alexa Weeks
2006	Madison	Alexa Weeks
2007	Sapphire	McLain Ward and Bluechip Bloodstock

Appendix D

AMERICAN GRAND PRIX ASSOCIATION RIDER OF THE YEAR

Year	Rider
1978	Melanie Smith
1979	Conrad Homfeld
1980	Conrad Homfeld
1981	Michael Matz
1982	Katie Monahan
1983	Leslie Burr
1984	Michael Matz
1985	Rob Gage
1986	Katie Monahan
1987	Rodney Jenkins
1988	Katie Monahan
1989	Margie Goldstein
1990	Hap Hansen
1991	Margie Goldstein
1992	Susan Hutchison
1993	Tim Grubb
1994	Margie Goldstein
1995	Margie Goldstein
1996	Margie Goldstein-Engle
1997	Beezie Patton

Appendix D

Year	Rider
1998	McLain Ward
1999	Margie Engle
2000	Margie Engle
2001	McLain Ward
2002	McLain Ward
2003	Margie Engle
2004	Beezie Madden
2005	Margie Engle
2006	Margie Engle
2007	McLain Ward

AMERICAN GRAND PRIX ASSOCIATION ROOKIE OF THE YEAR

Year	Rookie
1982	Louis Jacobs
1983	Jay Land
1984	Joie Gatlin
1985	Martha Wachtel
1986	Allana Featherstone
1987	Greg Best
1988	Lu Thomas
1989	Heather Fogerty
1990	Susanna Schroer
1991	McLain Ward
1992	Lise Quintero
1993	Barbie Bancroft
1994	Elizabeth Solter
1995	Laura Chapot
1996	Bjorn Ikast
1997	Kerry Bernay
1998	Stefanie Furgason
1999	Eliza Shuford
2000	Vanessa Haas
2001	Mark Watring

Year	Rookie
2002	Danielle Torano
2003	Michael Walton
2004	Derek Petersen
2005	Ellen Whitaker (GB)
2006	Janet Hirscher
2007	Cara Cheska

Appendix 7

SHOW JUMPING
HALL OF FAME INDUCTEES

Year	Inductees
1987	William Steinkraus
	Bertlan de Nemethy
	"Idle Dice"
1988	Patrick Butler
	August A. Busch Jr.
1989	David Kelley
	Jimmy Williams
	Ben O'Meara
	Frances Rowe
1990	Kathy Kusner
	Arthur McCashin
	Harry D. Chamberlin
	"San Lucas"
1991	Adolph Mogavero
	Whitney Stone
	Morton W. "Cappy" Smith
	Pat Dixon

Year	Inductees
1992	Eleonora "Eleo" Sears
	Mary Mairs Chapot
	Barbara Worth Oakford
	"Snowman"
1993	Dr. Robert C. Rost
	Joe Green
1994	Frank Chapot
	Gordon Wright
1995	Mickey Walsh
	"Trail Guide"
1996	Pamela Carruthers
	Dick Donnelly/"Heatherbloom"
	"Jet Run"
1997	Edward "Ned" King
	Bobby Egan/"Sun Beau"
1998	Melanie Smith Taylor
	Freddie Wettach Jr.
	Johnny Bell
1999	Rodney Jenkins
	Franklin F. Wing/"Democrat"
	"Sinjon"
2000	George Morris
	Carol Durand
	"Touch of Class"
2001	Bobby Burke
	Lieutenant John W. Russell
	Eugene R. Mische
	"Untouchable"
2002	Harry R. Gill
	Clarence L. "Honey" Craven
	"Calypso"
	"Gem Twist"
2003	J. Russell Stewart
	"Main Spring"
2004	"Snowbound"

Year	Inductees
2005	Michael Matz
	"For the Moment"
2006	Conrad Homfeld
2007	Joe Fargis
	Karen Golding
	Marcia "Mouse" Williams
2008	Dr. John Steele
	"Abdullah"
	"Miss Budweiser"
	"Riviera Wonder"
2009	"Balbuco"
	Neal Shapiro
2010	John Ammerman
	"Good Twist"
	Leonard King
2011	Jane Clark
	Gabor Foltenyi
	Hap Hansen
	Larry Langer
2012	"Starman"
	"Nautical"
	Jerry Baker
	Charles "Sonny" Brooks
2013	Steve Stephens
	Seamus Brady
	Daniel Marks, VMD

Appendix G
FEI World Cup Show Jumping Champions

Year	Rider	Country	Horse
1979	Hugo Simon	Austria	Gladstone
1980	Conrad Homfeld	United States	Balbuco
1981	Michael Matz	United States	Jet Run
1982	Melanie Smith	United States	Calypso
1983	Norman Dello Joio	United States	I Love You
1984	Mario Deslauriers	Canada	Aramis
1985	Conrad Homfeld	United States	Abdullah
1986	Leslie Burr Lenehan	United States	McLain
1987	Katharine Burdsall	United States	The Natural
1988	Ian Millar	Canada	Big Ben
1989	Ian Millar	Canada	Big Ben
1990	John Whitaker	Great Britain	Milton
1991	John Whitaker	Great Britain	Milton
1992	Thomas Frühmann	Austria	Genius
1993	Ludger Beerbaum	Germany	Ratina Z
1994	Jos Lansink	Netherlands	Libero H
1995	Nick Skelton	Great Britain	Dollar Girl
1996	Hugo Simon	Austria	E.T.

Year	Rider	Country	Horse
1997	Hugo Simon	Austria	E.T.
1998	Rodrigo Pessoa	Brazil	Baloubet du Rouet
1999	Rodrigo Pessoa	Brazil	Baloubet du Rouet
2000	Rodrigo Pessoa	Brazil	Baloubet du Rouet
2001	Markus Fuchs	Switzerland	Tinka's Boy
2002	Otto Becker	Germany	Dobel's Cento
2003	Marcus Ehning	Germany	Anka
2004	Bruno Broucqsault	France	Dileme de Cephe
2005	Meredith M.-Beerbaum	Germany	Shutterfly
2006	Marcus Ehning	Germany	Sandro Boy
2007	Beat Mändli	Switzerland	Ideo du Thot
2008	Meredith M.-Beerbaum	Germany	Shutterfly
2009	Meredith M.-Beerbaum	Germany	Shutterfly
2010	Marcus Ehning	Germany	Plot Blue and Noltes Küchengirl
2011	Christian Ahlmann	Germany	Taloubet Z
2012	Rich Fellers	United States	Flexible
2013	Beezie Madden	United States	Simon

Notes

Introduction

1. Marge Fernbacher, "The Horses' Week," *Plain Dealer*, July 22, 1977.

Chapter 1

2. John J. Grabowski, *Sports in Cleveland: An Illustrated History* (Cleveland, OH: Case Western Reserve University, 1992).

3. Christopher J. Eiben, *The Red-Hand Forever: The Hugh M. O'Neill Family of Cleveland, Ohio* (Cleveland, OH: O'Neill Brothers Foundation, 1997).

4. Grabowski, *Sports in Cleveland*.

5. Eiben, *Red-Hand Forever*.

6. Grabowski, *Sports in Cleveland*.

7. Laura J. Gorretta, *Chagrin Falls: An Ohio Village History* (Chagrin Falls, OH: Chagrin Falls Historical Society, 2004).

8. Ibid.

9. Alfred Mewett, "History of the First Cleveland Cavalry," Cleveland Spring Horse Show Program, May 1926.

10. David D. Van Tassel and John J. Grabowski, eds., *The Encyclopedia of Cleveland History*, 2nd ed. (Cleveland, OH: Case Western Reserve University, 1996).

Chapter 2

11. Grabowski, *Sports in Cleveland*.
12. Gates Mills Historical Society, *A Pictorial History of Gates Mills, 1826–1976* (Gates Mills, OH: Gates Mills Historical Society, 1976).
13. Diana Tittle and Mark Gottlieb, *Hunting Valley: A History* (Cleveland, OH: Hunting Valley Historical Society Inc., 1999).
14. Ibid.
15. Sandy Cobb, "Polo in the Chagrin Valley," *Moreland Hills Newsletter*, September 9, 2013.
16. Tittle and Gottlieb, *Hunting Valley*.

Chapter 3

17. J. Blan van Urk, *The Horse, the Valley and the Chagrin Valley Hunt* (New York: Richard Ellis, 1947).
18. The Cleveland Spring Horse Show Program, June 1930.
19. Show Jumping Hall of Fame and Museum Inc., Inductees 1987–2010.
20. Lake Erie College 1956–2006 Magazine Supplement (10–11).
21. Russell Township Historical Society, *Pictorial History of Russell Township* (Russell Township, OH: Russell Township Historical Society, 2010).
22. Official Program for the Fifteenth Annual Chagrin Valley Trails and Riding Club, 1964.
23. Ibid.
24. Ibid.
25. *The Chronicle of the Horse*, "The Cleveland Grand Prix," August 27, 1965.

Chapter 4

26. Major Louis A. DiMarco, "The Army Equestrian Olympic Team," www.LouisDiMarco.com.

Chapter 5

27. Betty Weibel, "A Look Back at the Birth of Grand Prix Show Jumping," KeyBank Hunter Jumper Classic CVPHA program, July 1996.

28. Candy Lawrence, "Andahazy Is Founding Father of Grand Prix," *The Times*, July 8, 1999.
29. Weibel, "A Look Back."
30. Lawrence, "Andahazy Is Founding Father."
31. Weibel, "A Look Back."
32. *The Chronicle of the Horse.*
33. Weibel, "A Look Back."
34. *The Chronicle of the Horse*, "The Cleveland Grand Prix," August 27, 1965.
35. Ibid.
36. Weibel, "A Look Back."

Chapter 6

37. Ibid.
38. Betty Weibel, "Cleveland Grand Prix Winner Memories," *Chagrin Valley PHA Program*, July 2005.
39. LaRue P. Daniels, "Grand Prix Is Show Stopper," *Plain Dealer*, July 21, 1967.
40. Max Riddle, "Gustavus Jumps into Favorite's Role," *Cleveland Press*, July 25, 1968.
41. *Times Leader*, "Canadian Jim Day Wins Grand Prix," July 29, 1968.
42. Marge Alge, "Grand Prix Honors Humphrey," *Cleveland Press*, July 15, 1968.
43. *New York Times*, "Illinois and Ohio Horse Shows Plagued by Violent Rain Storms," July 27, 1969.
44. Roland Kraus, "Canadian Winner in Cleveland Prix," *Plain Dealer*, July 28, 1969.

Chapter 7

45. *Plain Dealer*, "Toy Soldier Wins," July 26, 1970.
46. Ibid., "Act One Is Chagrin Gold Cup Champion," July 27, 1970.
47. Ibid., "Gold Cup Horse Shows Called Off," January 6, 1973.
48. Ibid., "Canadian Raps Splashdown, Quits Chagrin Valley Show," July 23, 1971.
49. Ibid., "Rosie Report Scores," July 31, 1972.
50. Ibid., "Springdale Scores Grand Prix Upset," July 30, 1973.
51. Ibid., "Show World Saddled with Rough Economy," September 26, 1975.
52. Ibid., "Sandsablaze Wins Prix," July 28, 1975.

53. *Cleveland Press*, "Jenkins Wins Two Prix Events—Rider Breaks Collarbone," July 30, 1977.

54. Show Jumping Hall of Fame induction news release, April 1, 2002.

55. "American Grand Prix Association and International Management Group Sign Marketing and TV Agreement," June 9, 1979.

Chapter 8

56. 1986 American Grand Prix Association media guide.

57. Betty Weibel, "Cleveland Key to Launching Debbie Stephens Grand Prix Career," CVPHA Program, July 2011.

58. Marge Fernbacher, "Former Clevelander Wins Prescott Grand Prix with Victory in Soggy Jump-Off," *Plain Dealer*, July 27, 1981.

Chapter 9

59. *Plain Dealer*, "Leone, Oxo Triumph Again, Win U.S. Open Jumping Title," July 22, 1991.

60. Ibid., "Goldstein Grand Prix Champion," July 13, 1992.

61. Ibid., "Hutchison Gallops to Victory," July 26, 1993.

62. Candy Lawrence, "Horse Shows Skip Valley—America's Oldest Grand Prix Cancelled," *Chagrin Valley Times*, May 12, 1994.

63. KeyBank Hunter Jumper Classic CVPHA news release, April 9, 1996.

64. Ibid., February 1, 1996.

65. *Chagrin Valley Times*, "Horse Show Expected to Kick Local Economy," July 5, 1996.

66. Ibid.

67. Ibid.

68. KeyBank Hunter Jumper Classic CVPHA news release, February 1, 1996.

69. CVPHA, "Goldstein-Engle Flies to Win at $30,000 KeyBank Cleveland Grand Prix," July 14, 1997.

70. Marge Fernbacher, "Amateur Steals Show, Wins KeyBank Jumping Title," *Plain Dealer*, July 13, 1998.

Chapter 10

71. Candy Lawrence, "Goldstein-Engle Adds to Grand Prix Total," *The Times*, July 20, 2000.

72. Ibid.

73. Tricia Booker, "Meet Course Designer Steve Stephens," KeyBank Hunter Jumper Classic CVPHA program, July 1999.

74. Chagrin Valley Hunter Jumper Classic program, "2001 Grand Prix Is Family Affair," July 2002.

75. Pete Gaughn, "Grand Prix Turns into Big Family Affair," *Sun Newspapers*, July 19, 2001.

76. Marge Fernbacher, "King Wins, Places, Shows—and More—at Grand Prix," *Plain Dealer*, July 15, 2002.

77. Dave Kich, "Another Engle Encore," *The Times*, July 21, 2005.

Chapter 11

78. Wachovia Securities American Gold Cup program, 2006.

79. "The American Gold Cup Moves to Cleveland in September 2006," Stadium Jumping news release, March 14, 2006.

80. Ibid.

81. Chagrin Valley Hunter Jumper Classic Souvenir program, July 2007.

82. AGA Progress Report, 1978–83.

Chapter 12

83. CVPHA, "Argentinian Federico Sztyrle Wins Welcome Stake and Cleveland Grand Prix," July 16, 2012.

84. Ibid., "19-year-old Shawn Casady Wins Welcome Stake and Cleveland Grand Prix," July 16, 2013.

85. Ibid., "Chagrin Valley Hunter Jumper Classic Expects to Raise Money For Local Charities," May 15, 2006.

86. Ibid.

87. CVPHA, "Cleveland Grand Prix Show Jumping Event Marks Landmark Achievement in Ohio's History," April 17, 2003.

INDEX

ABOUT THE AUTHOR

Betty Weibel is fortunate to have been able to combine her equestrian life with her career as a journalist and public relations professional. Early in her career, she oversaw public relations for the national American Grand Prix Association, managing media and sponsor relations for the thirty-event national series, as well as other

Author Betty Weibel with Ringmaster John Perry.

top show jumping events. Today, she is a principal in Yopko Penhallurick, a public relations agency that was instrumental in the Ohio Bicentennial celebration and received top national honors for its work. A graduate of Lake Erie College, she has served on the board of trustees for the Chagrin Valley PHA Horse Show, as well as a board member of Fieldstone Farm Therapeutic Riding Center and the Ohio Humanities Council. She lives with her family on a small horse farm in Geauga County, Ohio.